Advance Praise for
Teaching Them Young

"If you are a parent, this is one of the most important books you will read besides the Bible! Learning these principles will help you build a spiritual legacy in your children and grandchildren!"

Frank and Beverly Lum, *parents/grandparents*

"Dr. Betters' practical, real life examples challenge us to teach our children to see life through a Biblical worldview. As parents of young children, we found in this book instruction on keeping the gospel at the center of our family's life."

Kevin and Jen Smith, *parents*

"In a day when our young people are leaving the church in alarming numbers, Chuck Betters calls Christian parents back to the Biblical mandate to teach our children while they are young. The principles and promises of Proverbs come alive with practical stories, illustrations and strategies for passing our faith to the next generation."

Sue Jakes, *mother/grandmother, Education Specialist, Christian Education and Publications, Presbyterian Church in America*

"This book is chock full of vital information based on deep study of God's Word as well as Chuck's personal life experience. It is a gift from one generation to the next."

Sherry Bitler, *mother/grandmother, Children's Ministry Coordinator, Glasgow Reformed Presbyterian Church*

"Chuck has been our pastor for over twenty years. His insight and teaching have made the difference in the lives of all four of our children. Every godly parent needs to read this book."

Paul and Sue Palmer, *parents*

Teaching Them Young

The Hidden Treasures of the Proverbs

Dr. Chuck Betters

Teaching Them Young

Copyright © 2009 by Dr. Chuck Betters

New Heaven Publishing
P.O. Box 5711
Newark, DE 19714
(800) 655-2859
www.newheavenpublishing.com

Cover design by D3 Graphic Design

ISBN 13: 978-0-9793859-9-5
ISBN 10: 0-9793859-9-7

This book is dedicated to our fourteen grandchildren—
Cori, Markie, Danielle, Katie, Mollie, Benjamin, Emma,
Abby, Nathan, Caleb, C.J., Eva, Siddhi, and Samuel.
You are our legacy.

Acknowledgements

Raising children is difficult and requires a total commitment from both parents. Our children are walking with the Lord in ministry and are continuing the legacy with their children. For all of this, I will be forever grateful to my wife, Sharon, or as our grandchildren call her, Grammy. You are the heart and soul of our home, and my partner and completer for over forty years.

I am thankful for the wonderful people who, for over twenty three years, I have been privileged to serve, the saints at the Glasgow Reformed Presbyterian Church. Every pastor in his career should be able to serve in a church such as this one with leaders as Godly as the ones who guide our church. Thank you for encouraging me to write.

This book could not have been published without the countless hours dedicated to the project by Melane Bower, who organized the material from the "Teaching Them Young" sermon series.

And to my good friends, the father of our two daughters-in-law, Earle Gould, and his lovely wife Brenda, who tirelessly edited every chapter. Thank you and the dear mother of those girls, Judy, who is home with the Lord, for raising your girls on the principles contained in this book.

Table of Contents

Introduction

ONLY DAYS BEFORE our sixteen-year-old son, Mark, the youngest of our four children, was taken from us into heaven in a terrible car accident, he wrote a letter to me for my birthday. I did not know it existed until after his mother, my precious wife, Sharon, gave it to me on that very difficult first Christmas without Mark. What you are about to read are Mark's own lovingly written words, which have become the inspiration and motivation for this book. So, I want to offer both to you as instruction and encouragement for parents in the raising of their children on the timeless wisdom contained in the Bible's book of Proverbs:

Dad,

In all the years that you have been my father, there has not been a time when you failed to come through for me. There has not been a time when you failed to encourage me. You have always seen through me and my secretive ways and have not failed to counsel me when I need it most. The words, "You're wrong and I am right" are the words that I hate to hear the most, but I thank you for them. You are a dad that many kids only dream of having and I look up to you for all the knowledge that God has given you. I am proud to be called the "pastor's kid," because I believe it is worth dealing with all of the expecta-

tions that many people put on me. I thank God for you and the family He has given me each day. Any question that I ask, you have never failed to answer it. Any problem that I bring to you, you have never failed to help me through it. You have made sure that I am always happy and have never left me disappointed. Having you as my father is one of the best things God has given me. If I could repay you I would, but I know that is impossible. However, I can afford to tell you that I love you, and that I care about you very much.

Love,

Mark

This book is designed to glean eternal truths from the lips of Solomon as he gave urgent and loving instruction to his young son. In Jewish Old Testament life, children were raised to become men and women who feared God. They were expected, at a very young age, to memorize Scripture, celebrate the Holy feasts, embrace the one true God of Israel, and learn a trade by the time they were considered to be adults. Jewish parents were driven by a common and specific set of core values which they applied diligently in the raising of their children. And, by the time a child became a teenager and entered adulthood, it was expected that he or she would have embraced these same values. Then and only then, did a Jewish dad trust that his son or daughter was ready for the challenging life journey which lay ahead of them.

The words we use to describe a child's development—words such as *infant, toddler, pre-teen, teen, young adult,* and *adult*—have corresponding Hebrew equivalents. The premise of this book is that the first nine chapters of Proverbs were written by Solomon to his son before he had yet become a teenager. And, in these chapters, the common word used by this father when addressing his son, is a word describing a pre-teenager or a young child. Thus, it's clear that Solomon desired that his boy learn certain core principles before he reached the age of about thirteen. This is consistent with the Jewish cultural tradition that a young boy should demonstrate his knowledge of the Scriptures and be ceremonially declared a "man" when he reached the age of thirteen.

It is my fervent prayer that you will teach *your* children these principles before they are thirteen years old. There is certainly no magic associated with that age, but the longer it takes to instill these principles, the more difficult it becomes to reach your child for Christ. This is not to say God's power to save is limited by one's age. Nothing could be further from the truth. Yet it is a premise of this book, as well as that of many who have studied the development of the human personality, that a child's basic personality is formed by the time he or she is five years old. From that point forward, the kind of adult he or she becomes has, as its foundation, that basic, early personality.

But time is of the essence for another reason—namely that you, as parents, are not the only ones who are seeking to influence the hearts and minds of your children. From your child's earliest years in your home, the "information bombardment" begins. Whether it is music, TV, books, movies, visitors or your own adult conversations, your young child is watching and listening more than you may think. He is beginning to collect the rudimentary puzzle pieces that will form his worldview, and, more importantly, his "God view." Then, once he begins venturing outside your home to the playgrounds, the school yards and the malls, your opportunities to win his heart and convey life-dominating Godly principles will greatly diminish as peer pressure becomes a factor. In accordance with God's Wisdom and His loving design for the family, you are given the undivided attention and admiration of your child, as a "captive audience," only during those precious early years.

Grasp and treasure this opportunity with all of your heart and energy—and begin *teaching them young*!

Teaching Them Young is a challenging, yet rewarding, journey through these nine chapters of Proverbs, with the goal of extracting and applying those core values God wants your children to learn. This book is based on an extensive sermon series I preached by the same title. After hearing one of the sermons, a distraught young mother wept as she told my wife about how her eight-year-old son was treating her disrespectfully. She worried that, since he was already eight, she had only four more years to reach him. We assured her that this was not the case, but rather that parenting is a life-long marathon, not a sprint, and that successful parenting will only happen by God's Grace and not by some complicated magical formula. As faithful parents, we must take hope in the promise that the Godly principles embodied in the Proverbs, if lived and taught with consistency before our children, will find fertile ground in our children's lives (Isaiah 55:10 & 11).

As a grandfather to fourteen precious gems, I assure you that parenting is *never* finished. My wife and I still serve as a source of counsel and guidance for our adult children. I frequently remind them that our hope, as we were raising them, was that someday, when they are parents themselves, they would "do it better" than we did. That is precisely what has happened, and we gain great satisfaction in watching our children apply what they have learned. They have all married Godly spouses and are now raising their own children—and yes, they are "doing it better" than we did. Hopefully, as our legacy unfolds, their children will do it better than their parents did.

So, come along and take a journey with me through the gold mine that is the Proverbs, specifically, the first nine chapters. It is highly recommended that you listen to the "Teaching Them Young" sermon series along with the study of this book. This will add further perspective and help to maximize what you are able to take away with you

4

when our walk together is over. All of our resources are available through www.markinc.org.

CHAPTER ONE
The Fear of God and a Bucket Load of God-Esteem

Teach Your Children This Story

THERE ARE MANY speeches with memorable one-liners that have become the stuff of which folklore is made. For example, who of the "Greatest Generation" will ever forget Franklin Delano Roosevelt addressing Congress with these words: "Yesterday, December 7th, 1941, a date which will live in infamy, the United States of America was suddenly and deliberately attacked by naval and air forces of the Empire of Japan." Or who of the "Baby Boomer" generation can forget the words of President John F. Kennedy: "Ask not what your country can do for you—ask what you can do for your country." And what American, especially African-American, does not feel the electricity of hope and inspiration when they hear or see Dr. Martin Luther King's *I Have a Dream* speech?

But there are twelve words contained in a single speech that changed the course of human history and especially, post-Apostolic Christianity. On Halloween in 1517, Martin Luther nailed his *Ninety-Five Theses of Contention* ("Disputation of Dr. Martin Luther on the Power and Efficacy of Indulgences") to the church door at Wittenberg, accusing the Roman Catholic Church of heresy upon heresy. Along with other Reformers like John Wycliffe, John Hus, Thomas Linacre and John Colet, Luther put his life on the line for the cause of God and Truth. Luther's action was, in great part, a response to the selling of indulgences by Johann Tetzel, a Dominican priest. Luther directly challenged the position of the powerful and politically-savvy clergy in regard to individual salvation. Before long, Luther's *Ninety-Five Theses of Contention* had been copied and published all over Europe.

Martin Luther's Protestant views were condemned as heretical by Pope Leo X in 1520. He was subsequently summoned to either renounce or defend them at the Diet of Worms on April 17, 1521. There stood Luther, before that esteemed assembly. Johann von Eck, the assistant to the Archbishop of Trier, acted as spokesman for Emperor, Charles V. All of Luther's writings, including the Theses, were laid out before him on a table. Eck confronted Luther, demanding that he recant the message of those writings or face the wrath of the Church and the Emperor. When Martin Luther requested twenty-four hours to think about his answer, a shockwave rippled through the entire court assembly. How could this great spiritual leader of the Reformation movement be asking for more time? Was he actually caving under the pressure of *fear*?

Granted an extension, Luther spent the time in soul-wrenching prayer. When Johann von Eck presented the same demand to Luther the next day, the Reformer apologized for the harsh tone of many of his writings, but said that he could not recant them. Luther respectfully, but boldly, stated that "Unless I am convinced by proofs from Scriptures or by plain and clear reasons and arguments, I cannot and will not retract, for it is neither safe nor wise to do anything against conscience. Here I stand. I can do no other. God help me. Amen." Martin Luther's brief but immortal statement, "Here I stand," has, through the centuries, been inseparably and uniquely identified with the

Great Reformer himself. These words became the inspiration and the battle cry of the Reformation, and move Believers, to this day, to remember a man of conviction who stood alone before his powerful accusers and would not deny his Lord or compromise God's Holy Word—under threat of death. On May 25, the Emperor issued his Edict of Worms, declaring Martin Luther an "outlaw" and a "notorious heretic."

Luther was indeed fearful, but it was not a fear of his human accusers. He knew that his words would have a momentous impact on how God's plan of salvation would be made known to all people from that time onward. Many souls hung in the balance—more than he could have imagined at the time. He also knew that his response to von Eck's questioning touched upon the very nature of a Holy God and the sole authority of His inerrant Word. Luther knew that he would one day stand before that God and give an account for how he conducted himself. His words would forever condemn him as a heretic in the eyes of the Catholic Church and the Emperor.

We must be careful not to idolize or deify any of the Church's great figures of the past—or present, for they have feet of clay, as do all of us. But in that historic moment, Martin Luther's unwavering fear of his God trivialized any fear he felt of those who sought to destroy him. Once again, as in ancient times, an imperfect tool was used, with perfect timing, to expose error and refocus human hearts on the preeminence of the Scriptures *alone* in all matters relating to the nature of God and man's relationship to Him.

Parenting Principle: Raising Godly children begins by teaching them the fear of God.

> *The fear of the Lord is the beginning of knowledge, but*
> *fools despise wisdom and discipline.*
> Proverbs 1:7

My son, if you accept my words and store up my commands within you, turning your ear to wisdom and applying your heart to understanding, and if you call out for insight and cry aloud for understanding and if you look for it as for silver and search for it as for hidden treasure, then you will understand the fear of the Lord and find the knowledge of God.
Proverbs 2:1-5

To fear the Lord is to hate evil; I hate pride and arrogance, evil behavior and perverse speech.
Proverbs 8:13

King Solomon had it all. The legendary son of David and Bathsheba enjoyed a life that few others would ever experience—unimaginable wealth, great power, and an immeasurable amount of worldly possessions. His trading ships returned from distant lands overflowing with gold, silver and ivory (1 Kings 10:22), and he amassed a staggering collection of 1,400 chariots and 12,000 horses (1 Kings 10:26-29). With his resources, he built cities, palaces, and Israel's first temple. Both during his 40-year reign over a flourishing nation and as a standout figure in the annals of history, Solomon was one of the most revered rulers in Biblical times.

But despite his fortune, Solomon knew there had to be more than what the world had to offer. After years of searching for a deeper meaning in life, the great king finally came to one profound realization...

Now all has been heard; here is the conclusion of the matter: Fear God and keep his commandments, for this is the whole duty of man. For God will bring every deed into judgment, including every hidden thing, whether it is good or evil. (Ecclesiastes 12:13-14)

Similarly, the eternal measure of our own personal character, attributes, life goals and accomplishments can be evaluated with one simple question: *Do we fear God?* If we know Him, we must fear Him. There *will* come a time when we will all stand before God, whether in death or at His coming, and our works in this lifetime will be weighed. Those thoughts and deeds we presumed would be known only to us will, in fact, be exposed to the light of day; regardless of whether they are good or evil, we will all face a judgment rendered on the basis of a single standard— whether we feared God.

However, the fear of God cannot be measured only by the fear of judgment. God promises great reward to those who *rightly* fear Him in the Scriptural sense of the word. It's more likely our children will "catch" the fear of God when they observe the benefits such a fear produces in our own lives as parents. So since we cannot teach our children what we ourselves may not yet have learned, let's explore exactly what it means to fear God and how we can begin to experience the rewards He has promised.

The God-Fearing Person

In the New Testament, there were two ways in which a Gentile could convert to Judaism. He could become a righteous proselyte—that is, he would agree to be bound by all the doctrines, precepts and obligations of Old Testament Judaism, including circumcision, and was then considered to be a Jew in every practical sense of the word. Or he could become a gate proselyte, a resident alien who lived in Israel and adopted some of their customs and obligations. They were not required to be circumcised or to comply with all of the Laws in the Torah. These "converts" observed, to varying degrees, the Jewish system of worship and way of life but without becoming full proselytes. They were called, in the New Testament, *God-fearers*.

Out of a combination of expedience and reason, the God-fearers came to reject the polytheism of the surrounding culture and embrace Israel's monotheism because they feared they might offend the one true God whom they had heard about. While a proper fear of God will certainly deliver us from the fear of men, as we learned from the story of Martin Luther's trial, there are other elements that come into play. An integral part of a true, Biblical fear of God is a solemn, speechless awe for what He has done *for* us as much as it is a bone-chilling terror for what He could do *to* us if we ever were to become the object of His wrath.

Since the fear of God is the very beginning of knowledge (Proverbs 1:7) and the central motivation for hating evil (Proverbs 8:13), it is clearly essential that we have our children thoroughly understand the Scriptural meaning of "the fear of God":

•   Fearing God means to be in complete and total awe of His character and nature, as well as holding a deep and abiding reverence for Him. Jewish tradition honored God so highly that they wouldn't dare to speak His name aloud or even write out all the letters of His name. Even to this day, many deeply-observant and Orthodox Jews will write out the name of God as, "G*D." His name was too Holy to even touch the lips of sinful man.

•   Fearing God also means we are anxious to please the One who loves us more than anyone else ever could. When we fear God, we fear the possibility of dishonoring, disappointing, or disobeying Him.

•   When we fear God in the right way, we begin to truly understand His love, and evidence a humble gratitude toward Him as a result.

It is impossible to learn the fear of God without also understanding the ethical demands of Scripture. One of the most important lessons that the book of Proverbs teaches us is that God gives us Wisdom through His Word (*logos*) and that we must internalize Biblical truth in order to consistently put it into practice. To raise a child who knows, loves, and fears God requires a balance of Wisdom and practical application (understanding). We must teach them that God indeed has laws and precepts that are driven by His love for us and are for our good...

"If you accept my words and store up my commands within you, turning your ear to wisdom and applying your heart to understanding, and if you call out for insight and cry aloud for understanding, and if you look for it as silver and search for it as hidden treasure, then you will understand the fear of the LORD and find the knowledge of God." (Proverbs 2:1)

When we store up the Word of God through disciplined study, we are in fact downloading a cache of hidden treasures that can never be obtained casually. In other words, we must seek these riches *diligently*. When our children download the Word of God into their soul's spiritual computer, they will be prepared to upload it into any situation at the time and place they need it most. The Word of God, implanted into a child's heart, is like kegs of time-delayed dynamite charges, ready to detonate when they are face to face with the crises and demonic assaults that they will inevitably face in life.

Everything God wants us to know about His character and nature has been made known to us in the person of His Son, Jesus Christ, the incarnate Word—the *Logos*...

In the beginning was the Word, and the Word was with God, and the Word was God. He was with God in the beginning...And the Word became flesh and made his dwelling among us. We have seen his glory, the glory of the One and Only, full of grace and truth. (John 1:1, 14)

Everything God was, is, or ever will be (*Logos*) has been revealed to us in the person of Jesus Christ, at least to the extent of our limited human understanding. And, Jesus is the *Logos* incarnate (made flesh). God became a man who came to save His people from their sins. This glorious plan of salvation has been recorded in one book with sixty-six chapters, the Holy Scriptures. Everything God wants us to know about Him has been written down and preserved by the Holy Spirit (John 14:26). All the primary resources you need to successfully raise your child to be a remarkable Christian, a great worker, and a dedicated kingdom-builder who knows, loves, and fears God, have been handed to you on the golden tablets of the Bible.

As a younger parent struggling with the many challenges of raising young children, my peers would often say, only half-jokingly, "I sure wish newborn babies came with an instruction manual!" Well, they do! And I'll wager you have at least one copy in your home. Isn't it time to see what the "manufacturer" has to say?

Many child-rearing professionals today arguably teach that the basic personality of a child is formed by the time he or she reaches five years of age. The rest of their lives will be built, in one way or another, for better or for worse, upon that pre-shaped personality. This is curiously similar to what The Manufacturer's Instruction Manual says: *Train a child in the way he should go, and when he is old he will not turn from it* (Proverbs 22:6).

If we learn early what it means to raise our children on the Proverbs, we would understand that the *fear of God* is the core element, foundational to the entire book. It is when we discover the fear of God that we are equipped to glorify God and enjoy Him forever—the chief end of man.

Few people in modern America have raised their children with a practical understanding of the Proverbs. And we are all sadly aware that our once God-honoring public school system has now forbidden even the brief reading of a verse or two from the Bible at the beginning of each day. So, as unthinkable as it may seem, we are just one generation removed from those who have never even *heard* of the Proverbs—as a matter of fact, we may already be there! We desperately need to affirm our commitment to the teaching of Wisdom and the practical learning of the fear of God. With that in mind, let's examine several concepts that will help us reach that goal with our children.

The Fear of the Father

*These are the commands, decrees and laws the Lord
your God directed me to teach you to observe in the
land that you are crossing the Jordan to possess,
so that you, your children and their children after them
may fear the Lord your God as long as you live by
keeping all his decrees and commands that I give you,
and so that you may enjoy long life.*
Deuteronomy 6:1-6

For the myriad of families throughout our culture, the growing rate of absentee fathers has become a tragically significant factor in the lack of Biblical instruction in the home. Over twenty-five million children live apart from their biological fathers—that's one out of every three children in America. Nearly two out of three African-American children and four out of ten Hispanic children live in absentee-father homes. Without a highly involved father in the home, children are much more at risk for substance abuse[1] and are more likely to drop out of school.[2] When they reach adolescence they are twice as likely to become involved in early sexual activity and seven times more likely to become pregnant.[3]

The crisis of the absentee father is one of the greatest social ills that we're facing today and it has affected the evangelical church as a whole. Without fathers to protect and lead the family, children are more likely to reject parental authority. Simply put, a child learns to rightly fear God the Father when they learn to rightly fear their earthly fathers—using the word *fear* in the context of the Scriptural definition I discussed earlier.

We need dads who are committed to teaching their children the Scriptures, but dads can only effectively pass on that which they themselves possess. Thus, only men who fear God are equipped to teach their children to fear God. We need a generation of men who understand that the most important thing they can do for their children is to wholeheartedly pursue their own relationship with God and to immerse themselves in the quest to teach those children the fear of God. We need fathers who are equipped to hold themselves up to their children as role models and heroes, showing them how to practically live out the fear of God, one day at a time.

Fathers, this role cannot be delegated to anyone else—not the Church, not the school, and not your spouse. As a man of God, you must be willing to stand committed to Christ, unashamed of the Gospel before your children, while at the same time be willing to demonstrate the true strength of character that readily, but appropriately, admits to sin, weaknesses and failures. To hypocritically hide behind a façade of infallibility and pride will only breed resentment in both your wife and your children.

The Myth of Self-Esteem

"I'm OK...you're OK...we're OK."
"Let your conscience be your guide."
"Be true to yourself."
"You must love yourself first."
"It's all about me!"

These are the sermons the high priests and priestesses of New Age-ism and secular progressivism—the secular media and the public education system—preach from their pulpits. The truth is that this humanistic brand of self-esteem is twisted and dangerous. Humanistic self-esteem actually encourages a love of self that, once it has taken hold, naturally produces a reactionary hatred for the things of God.

Man was created to worship his Creator. When the focus of worship shifts (out of pride) from God to man himself, God, by definition, becomes the enemy. The things we love so much about ourselves—our emotions, our will, and our intellect—have been infected by our deadly sin nature and are therefore suspect when applied to the daily circumstances of our lives. This is at the heart of what I call the "Pauline double talk." You may need to read this very slowly to catch Paul's frustration with his inner self.

We know that the law is spiritual; but I am unspiritual, sold as a slave to sin. I do not understand what I do. For what I want to do I do not do, but what I hate I do. And if I do what I do not want to do, I agree that the law is good. As it is, it is no longer I myself who do it, but it is sin living in me. I know that nothing good lives in me, that is, in my sinful nature. For I have the desire to do what is good, but I cannot carry it out. For what I do is not the good I want to do; no, the evil I do not want to do—this I keep on doing. Now if I do what I do not want to do, it is no longer I who do it, but it is sin living in me that does it. So I find this law at work: When I want to do good, evil is right there with me. For in my inner being I delight in God's law; but I see another law at work in the members of my body, waging war against the law of my mind and making me a prisoner of the law of sin at work within my members. What a wretched man I am! Who will rescue me from this body of death? Thanks be to God—through Jesus Christ our Lord! So then, I myself in my mind am a slave to God's law, but in the sinful nature a slave to the law of sin. (Romans 7:14-25)

Huh? What did he say? He sounds frustrated. He, in essence, said that our children are not to fall in love with themselves or trust the "inner spark of goodness and decency in the hearts of all humans." Quite the contrary, their "self" stands against the nature and character of a Holy

God. To encourage self-love without Biblical constraint implies that our children are naturally good and can safely obey the dictates of their conscience. But we are all born sinners (Romans 3:23), and when we encourage a child in self-love we're actually appealing to their most base and sinful nature.

Self-love, as well as its humanist cousins, self-image and self-esteem, leads to faulty moral decision-making. Bad choices and self-love go hand-in-hand. When faced with a moral decision, I can either appeal to my inner man, that is, who I really am inside: a sinful, depraved human being, or to the Word of God. If I am in love with myself, namely, my flesh, and my sinful inner man, then all that I do will be tainted with pride and self-serving motives. This is Paul's frustration. He wants to do the right thing but there is a raging war within. To encourage this sort of self-love is to drive our children to believe that they can make all manner of selfish choices without consequences—after all, "You deserve it!" Such a child quickly realizes that he is in control and life in the home now becomes a real challenge. As parents, we must teach our children that choices and consequences go hand-in-hand.

Rather than working to encourage this flesh-driven brand of self-esteem in our children, we need to pump them up with a bucket full of "God-esteem." Helping them to understand their identity in Christ—teaching them how He loves them and how they are to love Him, and know they can claim righteousness through His atoning sacrifice—will give them the opportunity to cultivate and choose a true, Biblical self-esteem that no amount of peer pressure will ever be able to destroy. In fact, instilling and emphasizing worldly self-esteem arms Satan with the perfect tool of pride by which to appeal to your child's basest, self-serving instincts. Beware, we adults are not immune either.

We would truly be stranded in a state of dark hopelessness if the Apostle Paul had left us with the cry of his soul for help and deliverance: "*What a wretched man I am! Who will rescue me from this body of death?"* (Romans 7:24)

But take a look at how he confidently answers his own question:

"Thanks be to God–through Jesus Christ our Lord!" (Romans 7:25)

Therefore, there is now no condemnation for those who are in Christ Jesus, because through Christ Jesus the law of the Spirit of life set me free from the law of sin and death. (Romans 8:1-2)

This is a man with a bucket load of God-esteem.

The Meaning of Discretion

According to Webster's *Revised Unabridged Dictionary*, *discretion* is defined as "wise conduct and management; cautious discernment, especially as to matters of propriety and self-control; prudence; circumspection; wariness." The Oxford American Dictionary adds, "keeping secrets" (or able to be trusted with a confidence) and "good judgment."

Throughout the Proverbs, Solomon repeatedly prays that God would give him "discretion." But what does he mean? What is he looking for? How will he know if God answers this prayer? If our children are to be successful and make Godly choices for their lives, they must learn the meaning of this important word.

The Christian faith is not just a series of negative rules and prohibitions. Someone who has cultivated a strong Judeo-Christian worldview craves Biblical restraint in his life. Kids actually crave clear boundaries, and are happiest when their limits are well defined. This may surprise you since, so often, our children seem driven to challenge their parents and step outside the boundaries. Show me a child throwing a temper-tantrum and I will show you a child who likely has no clear boundaries or has not learned submission to boundaries. This, in part, is what Paul meant when he established some key disciplinary constraints for both children and their parents:

Children, obey your parents in the Lord, for this is right. "Honor your father and mother"--which is the first commandment with a promise—"that it may go well with you and that you may enjoy long life on the earth." Fathers, do not exasperate your children; instead, bring them up in the training and instruction of the Lord. (Ephesians 6:1-4)

Several modern English dictionaries combine to give a range of related definitions for Paul's carefully chosen verb, *exasperate*: to "greatly irritate, incense, anger, provoke and increase intensity of violence."

One surefire way to exasperate your child is to leave him devoid of boundaries. Teaching our children Godly morals and the meaning of discretion requires that they have a role model to follow. Most kids will imitate their parents. When children lack a moral compass, it is often because they have not observed the practical *instruction* and *discipline* in basic Biblical morality flowing from parents who are living examples. Many parents lose sight of this obligation in their quest for worldly success, both for themselves and for their children. Good grades, a college education and a lucrative career are admirable goals. But, any day, give me a low-income, blue-collar parent with limited formal education, who truly loves and fears God and is firmly grounded in Christ, over a parent who has a 4.0 grade point average, a degree in rocket science, and who is determined to live their life in open animosity toward God and to influence their family to do likewise.

Teaching our children the boundaries of the Christian life is a 24-7 task:

Love the Lord your God with all your heart and with all your soul and with all your strength. These commandments that I give you...are to be upon your hearts. Impress them on your children. Talk about them when you sit at home and when you walk along the road, when you lie down and when you get up. (Deuteronomy 6:5-7)

A Judeo-Christian worldview is the grid through which we ought to view life. It will orient our thinking and sharpen our perspective when we read world headlines, when we make life choices such as whom we will marry, when we make financial decisions, when we choose the values by which we will raise our children, and even when we vote. But, what are the necessary ingredients that comprise a Biblical worldview? According to the Proverbs, a Judeo-Christian worldview is driven and motivated by the fear of God, informed by the Word of God, and practically implemented with Holy discretion. As Paul reminded us in Romans 7, our thinking must be validated by our actions – actions that speak loudly about how we live out that worldview in our practical day-to-day lives.

This is the meaning of the word *discretion*. It is the means by which we translate our worldview into action. Discretion is Holy Spirit driven and guides the process by which we apply the Word of God to our daily circumstances. Since the Wisdom of God, in the person of the Holy Spirit, indwells all who know Christ, the committed Christian has a giant head start in collecting the ingredients to fill his bucket of God-esteem. So here are the ingredients:

• *Personal Relationship to Jesus*: Your child must come to know Christ early—the earlier the better.

• *Holy Spirit Power*: When your child meets Jesus, he or she is filled with the Holy Spirit and thus possesses the Wisdom of God and the capacity to demonstrate it.

• *Commitment to God's Word*: God has made His mind known to us in His written Word.

- *Planting God's Word in our Hearts*: As you teach your children from the Word of God, and they commit it to their hearts, precept upon precept, they store up for action the weapons of spiritual warfare.
- *Biblical Worldview*: As they mature in their understanding of God's Word, your children will learn to think Biblically, that is, they will embrace the Judeo-Christian worldview.
- *Practical Application of God's Word*: When faced with temptation or testing of any kind, your child must learn the rules of engagement, that is, to be filled or empowered by the Holy Spirit, and act according to the Word of God.

This is the meaning of *discretion*.

And this is what the *Shemma* (the Hebrew term for the life-dominating exhortation of Deuteronomy 6:5-7) is all about. Whether our children are coming out or going in, it is our responsibility to always remind them of these commandments, and to make sure that they are bound to our children's hearts. Some might call this "brainwashing," but, if our brains are dirty, they need a good cleaning! And if you don't take the initiative to positively "program" your children's hearts and minds with God's precepts, there are others out there who are eager to do their own "programming" in your place.

Preparation for Moral Choices

My son, do not forget my teaching,
but keep my commands in your heart.
Proverbs 3:1

It is a serious blow to successful parenting to allow our children to make their own choices without also helping them beforehand to develop the convictions and Godly judgment necessary to make those choices. In Proverbs 3:1, Solomon passionately implores his son to remember his father's words, because the young boy would surely need them one day. Without a doubt, that child would someday be faced with situations and temptations that would require him to draw upon the wisdom of his father to help see him through.

Don't wait until your children are adolescents to discuss with them the likelihood that friends will try to influence them by using bad language, lying (especially to parents), keeping secrets from their parents, watching certain movies, drinking alcohol, smoking, sneaking around, stealing, taking drugs, watching pornography, or having sexual relations. And this is by no means an exhaustive list, as you might imagine. Look for opportunities in your home, on the playground, in play groups, and during bedtime talks to teach them while they're young.

I recall one incident years ago, when our two junior-high aged sons, Dan and Mark, were invited to a party. Their mom and I both knew there was something amiss when, just before the party, Sharon called the host's mother and she informed us that she had been given strict orders by her daughter not to come down to the basement once the party had started (as if *that* wasn't a dead give-away—keeping secrets!).

We realized ahead of time that, although it would be messy, this would be a tremendous teaching moment. After enduring much begging, we chose to allow the boys to go to the party. The line would be let out just a bit to see how the fish would bite! When we picked them up several hours later, they looked like two scared rabbits as they quietly slipped into the car. Although they were prepared for what they might face that night at the party, because we had warned them, our sons now *knew* that they had been in the wrong place. They felt awkward and embarrassed being in our presence—an entirely proper "fear of father" and fear of God. But we had pre-armed them with everything they needed to properly deal with that situation.

Here was our teaching moment. We wanted our children to see, just as we had warned them, that they could quickly, as if by ambush, find themselves in the wrong place with the wrong people who would tempt them to do the wrong things. After a lengthy discussion and a review of the Biblical principles that had been violated— principles we taught them—they got it, and we knew they got it. They had "failed forward" in our presence, and we were proud of their willingness to admit their fault and talk about their flawed thinking process.

As our children were growing up, they weren't at liberty to choose their own friends—that responsibility belonged to us. It was up to us to test the chemistry of their friendships, and that even included Christians whose parents were *our* friends. We recognized early on that some personalities do not mix well when it comes to making moral choices together. When our children returned from spending time with another child and our task of parenting suddenly became more difficult, we knew we had to limit that relationship. We didn't blame the other child or their parents, but we accepted the fact that our child was not ready, or grown up enough, to make appropriate choices in the context of that friendship. These were painful decisions for our children, but were also teaching moments where we held them responsible for making poor choices that had consequences.

The importance of having an active role in the friendship question is based on the principle that your children's friends should *never* be their teachers. We know that we must aggressively guard our children from exposure to the counsel of the ungodly. Childhood peer pressure is one of the most forceful influences for bad behavior, so why would any responsible parent *not* want to keep close watch over this aspect of their child's life! The Proverbs tell us that...

Folly is bound up in the heart of a child (Proverbs 22:15).

When you look at your children's friends, it is reasonable to conclude that *this child is a fool, just as my child is a fool.* So, when your children's friends become their teachers, the result is what? The blind leading the blind—fools teaching fools! Dangerous chemistry!

Balancing Truth and Grace

My son, do not despise the Lord's discipline and do not resent his rebuke, because the Lord disciplines those he loves, as a father the son he delights in.
Proverbs 3:11-12

One of the most powerful ways your child will grow in the fear of God is to teach them the delicate balance between Truth and Grace—the bookends of tender, loving discipline. When our children were caught doing something seriously wrong, I would sit down with them, pray with them, instruct them as to how their behavior violated God's Word, and with the trusty old wooden spoon in my hand, they knew full well that they were about to face some serious discipline.

There we would sit, face to face, no anger, no screaming or yelling (most of the time). I would lead them to answer a series of questions, using language appropriate for their age: "What did you do?" "What Biblical principle did you violate?" "How have you offended God?" "How have you offended your parents?" "How could you commit this sin against your God who loves you so much?" These are "what" type questions rather than "why" type questions. The latter only invites excuses; the former gets to the heart of both the child and the offense.

We would then discuss the consequences—what punishment they could expect. "Do you know what you deserve? You've offended God, you've offended me, and you've offended your mother. Now you must face the consequences. However, this time, I'm going to show you the meaning of the word *Grace*. The debt is canceled. I will show you Grace and Mercy. This is precisely what Christ did on the cross for you." This meant they weren't going to get that well-deserved spanking (or whatever punishment was commensurate with the crime, since spanking must always be the last resort). Of course, this didn't happen all the time, but it happened frequently enough that we could effectively teach our children the balance between Truth and Grace. And an equally valuable lesson has been taught—the child cannot be permitted, when caught misbehaving, to take off down the path of denial, lying, excuse-making and blame-shifting—all natural responses in a child as well as adults. This makes a parent's future disciplinary "encounters" a bit easier, and prepares the child to become a discretionary, God-fearing adult.

Of course, God's Grace and Mercy transcend any we might demonstrate in that, unlike the child who has been spared the wrath of his dad, Jesus incurred the full weight of the punishment for our sins so that we would not have to. This is precisely how God withholds punishment from us. The punishment for our sins was laid on Jesus who bore in His flesh the equivalent of an eternity in hell for our sins. This is the meaning of pure Grace and Mercy.

The fear of God in your children begins with *you*, and whether or not you have trusted Him to frame the boundaries of your life. That's really the question, isn't it? Doesn't it all begin with *your* fear of God? The fear of God is what truly determines our success in this life—not money, education, or power. Success is measured by whether our children walk with, know, love and fear God. It all begins with us as parents.

Teaching Moments

• Teach your children the stories of the great heroes of faith such as Martin Luther, John Hus, and the Martyrs. Purchase *Foxe's Book of Martyrs*. Read the stories and retell them to your children with age-appropriateness in mind. Doing this will help your child learn about other people who had also come to know, love, and fear God.

• Use a variety of symbols during family worship—a cross, a crown of thorns, pictorial Bibles, or even a home-made whip made out of rope and bone chips—to illustrate to your children the majesty of God and what love cost Him.

• Using a telescope (or going to a Planetarium) will enable you to explore the wonders of creation and the power and transcendence of an Almighty God. This will be a great time to teach your children that, although this God is "wholly other," He is also immanent, that is, He is everywhere throughout the universe yet He knows them and has loved them personally.

• Television can be a very effective tool for identifying possible situations where they will face some tough moral choices. Record their favorite programs and, while playing them back, pause and ask them about scenes they just witnessed: "What did that little boy just say or do?" "Was he right or wrong about the choice he made?" "What do you think of that?" "What does *God* think of that?" It drove our kids crazy when we interrupted their shows that way, but it was an ideal way to help instill in them the values we knew they had to learn.

• Rediscover the family dinner table. The dinner hour is a time to sit down together and discuss the events of the day. When you ask them how their day went, do not accept "fine" or "OK" as an answer. Ask them for five examples of exactly what they meant when they said "fine" or "OK"! Every night, we seized those critical teaching moments to help reinforce the values that would help them continue to make the right choices as they grew older.

• Role playing is another excellent way of helping your child understand the potential situations he or she will face, and how to effectively respond to them. *Daniel resolved not to defile himself with the royal food and wine, and asked the chief official for permission not to defile himself this way* (Daniel 1:8). He made that decision *before* he got there, and probably even role-played it in his head. You could set up an imaginary scenario in which your children are challenged by a "friend" to spend an afternoon stealing from stores at the mall. How should they respond? What should they say or do? Discuss how to respond in each instance, and refer to appropriate Scriptures as reinforcement.

- A recent survey among middle and high school teens revealed some frightening trends in their moral decision-making ability. Visit this website, http://oasis.state.ga.us/oasis/yrbs/index.asp and then discuss the survey questions that are age appropriate to gain insight into how your child is thinking.

- Soak in these Scriptures (use several translations to get the full meaning) that reveal God's promises to those who fear Him. Memorize several with your child: Psalm 34:7, 2 Kings 17:39; Psalm 25:14; Psalm 147:11; Psalm 103:13, 17; Psalm 111:10; Job 28:28; Proverbs 14:27; Proverbs 19:23; Psalm 33:18.

---

[1] Bronte-Tinkew, Jacinta, Kristin A. Moore, Randolph C. Capps, and Jonathan Zaff. "The influence of father involvement on youth risk behaviors among adolescents: A comparison of native-born and immigrant families." Article in Press. Social Science Research, December 2004.

[2] U.S. Department of Health and Human Services. National Center for Health Statistics. Survey on Child Health. Washington, D.C.: GPO, 1993

[3] Ellis, Bruce J., John E. Bates, Kenneth A. Dodge, David M. Ferguson, L. John Horwood, Gregory S. Pettit, and Lianne Woodward. "Does Father Absence Place Daughters at Special Risk for Early Sexual Activity and Teenage Pregnancy." Child Development 74 (May/June 2003): 801-821

CHAPTER TWO
Raising a Spiritual Dropout

Teach Your Children This Story

BY THE END of the summer Olympic Games in 1992, the name Derrick Redmond would be forever branded in the hearts and minds of millions of people throughout the world.

It wasn't because the man was an exceptional athlete, although he did hold the British record for the 400-meter sprint and had already captured several gold medals in worldwide competitions. But in spite of his relatively successful career as a track runner, Derrick had been plagued by a series of injuries that were constantly interrupting his rise to stardom. The fact that he had even made it to the Olympics was surprising to many; Derrick had already endured over 22 surgeries on his Achilles tendon, and it seemed to be a miracle that he was able to walk, let alone run.

After much hard work and dedication, Derrick's Olympic "moment in the sun" finally arrived. He would run the 400-meter semi-final, and when it was over, his hope was that he would add another medal—preferably gold—to his collection. But only a minute into the race, Derrick felt searing pain suddenly shoot through his leg as his hamstring snapped. He crumbled onto the track, writhing in pain as the other runners sped past him.

The moment seemed suspended in time as Derrick finally sat up, paused to look over his shoulder, and then turned to look ahead. His face contorting with pain, he struggled to his feet and began limping down the track toward the finish line, brushing away trainers who suddenly appeared beside him to offer help. Moments later, to the crowd's astonishment, his father, Jim Redmond, sprinted onto the track, slipped his arm around his son's waist for support, and helped him limp across the finish line in last place as a standing ovation from 65,000 onlookers thundered throughout the stadium.

Derrick Redmond's story reminds me of the vital life message that I seek to always impress upon my children and grandchildren: *finish well.*

Parenting Principle: Emotional bondage produces spiritual quitters.

Do you ever hear inner voices?

Like most other readers, your answer is probably "no!" But if I told you that your *child* hears voices every day of his or her life, what would you say?

The fact is that your child *does* hear voices...voices that are sometimes loud and at other times nothing more than soft whispers. They are voices that cunningly entice our children to wander down the pathway to moral failure...voices reaching out from the pit of hell itself. We are engaged in a life-and-death struggle against demonic powers (Ephesians 6:12; 1 Peter 5:8), and this truth must be impressed upon your children.

We live in a world that has abandoned a traditional Judeo-Christian worldview of morality and has redefined what is and what is not "moral failure." For several generations now, the boundary lines of morality have drifted so far that, like frogs in a kettle, we, as a society, have been slowly dying a moral death—and many parents do not even realize what's been happening. Things that were once considered immoral—immodest dress, divorce, pre-marital sexual relations, unwed pregnancies, abortion, homosexuality, and more are commonplace in today's culture. Each and every one of us, including our children, lives within the personal context of such temptations. Knowingly dashing down the road that leads to moral failure is now all too easy in our many unguarded moments, especially if our moral compass is broken.

I believe that this failure begins with three key, emotionally charged sin patterns, bound up in the heart of every child that, if not mastered, can contribute to the likelihood of moral failure in his or her life: they are fear, selfishness, and pride. Finishing our earthly race well (Hebrews 12:1) requires our addressing these patterns throughout our lives, starting in childhood.

Fear contributes to emotional bondage.

When you lie down, you will not be afraid; when you lie down, your sleep will be sweet. Have no fear of sudden disaster or of the ruin that overtakes the wicked; for the Lord will be your confidence and will keep your foot from being snared. (Proverbs 3:24-26)

We extensively discussed the fear of God in Chapter 1, but there is another type of fear that should be addressed with your child: the fear of the uncontrollable and the unknown. What starts out as a youthful fear of monsters in the closet can evolve, over time, into a fear of non-acceptance by his peers, the fear of failure, or even a fear of intimacy and commitment as he grows older. Parents, have your fear radar switched on at all times and take careful notice of the signals your children may be sending that suggest they're struggling with some form of fear.

Childhood fears come in all shapes and sizes. What is it about bedtime that brings them out from their dark hiding places? Sharon and I tried to respond to these fears with sensitivity, sometimes "killing" invisible spiders or chasing monsters from the room. Other fears deserved more serious attention. Our daughter, Heidi, vividly remembers the night she tearfully came into our bedroom, terrified of being alone. Visions of the end of the world depicted in a religious movie that we had seen at the Sunday evening service, evoked terror that refused to go away. My efforts to calm her were fruitless. Our usually sensible daughter could not be settled, so I climbed into bed with her that night so that she could sleep. Though I didn't plan it, I believe that simple act of acknowledging her fear and coming alongside her went a long way in encouraging our adolescent daughter that her Daddy would always protect her.

We seldom manage to completely overcome these fears, but when faced with them, we all will react in one of two ways: we either control them or they control us. Some men act out their fears in the form of uncontrolled anger, a trait that reflects the young boy deep within who is still struggling for ways to deal with his fears. Some women subconsciously express their fears by compulsively attempting to control or manipulate their environment, making sure that everything around them is orderly and fits properly in its place. This kind of behavior may suggest a fear of insecurity. Both instances are the result of deep-rooted fears that were very likely never handled or mastered during the pre-teen years.

Some children are more fearful than others, so parents must know their child's unique personality as they prepare them for life. If children do not learn early on how to handle fear, then it will most likely control them for the rest of their lives. In order to help our children overcome this sort of fear, we must teach them that God is their refuge and strength (Psalm 46:1), no matter how frightening life becomes or how many fearful decisions they will have to make. They must learn and understand that the Lord is their God when they are asleep or awake, and that He is always holding them firmly in the grip of His loving Grace. Even when they feel He is distant or has abandoned them, we want our children to choose to believe that God would never leave or forsake them. (Hebrews 13:5)

I lift up my eyes to the hills—where does my help come from? My help comes from the Lord, the Maker of heaven and earth. He will not let your foot slip—he who watches over you will not slumber; indeed, he who watches over Israel will neither slumber nor sleep. (Psalm 121:1-4)

Fear can be a life-dominating emotion that, if not mastered, can act as the central influence in the many choices we will be faced with in our lives. Moral balance, a genuine knowledge of right and wrong, is achieved when we learn to frame our doings, establish moral boundaries, and truly recognize when moral restraint is called for. When we are overtaken by fear, we lose our spiritual perspective. The balance tips—and it usually tips toward moral failure.

Selfishness contributes to emotional bondage.

Folly is bound up in the heart of a child.
Proverbs 22:15

Years ago, our two youngest sons, Dan and Mark, shared a dream of becoming rock stars. Bent on the pursuit of stardom, the boys often spent their days and nights in the basement of our home, making music with the "rock band" they had formed together with the boy next door. Their marathon rehearsals were usually interrupted only after I could not take it anymore, switched off the basement lights, and announced that "this session is now over." The music would stop, silence would fill the darkened basement, and no one protested my action. Without a doubt, our sons and their friends knew that when the lights went out, rehearsal was over for the day. They were learning that parents set boundaries and that arguing would likely net them more trouble.

Although I knew full well that neither of them was going to become the kind of rock star they hoped to be (because I wasn't going to let them), I also knew that it was important for them to flap their wings and exercise their musical gifts—while I, as their father, stayed close and guarded the boundaries of their lives. So when their band managed to book a concert at a local church, I agreed to run the sound system (even though I disliked their music) for the momentous event. My wife and I were willing to experience personal inconvenience (in this case, window-rattling drum sessions) so that our children felt safe pursuing their hobbies in our presence. In turn we were able to monitor their activities and friendships.

As it turned out, the band performed *miserably* at this concert. In fact, as the boys later admitted, they were so terrible that our oldest son, Chuck—who now holds his doctorate in worship and is a classically trained concert pianist—begged me during the performance to turn the sound off. I refused. They were failing, yes, but they were failing in front of us, that is, they were "failing forward." They failed without their parents' ridicule or condemnation, which would have only served to pour salt on their wounds and thus jeopardize any future "failing forward."

To borrow their words, they "stunk up the place." The boys knew how badly they had failed, as did everyone else who heard them. They all climbed meekly into our car after the concert was over, none of them saying a word until we were about halfway home, when I finally heard someone in the back seat mumble a resigned confession: "We were awful, weren't we...?" They didn't need me to say a word—not even, "I told you so!"—at least not this time.

I tell you this story to illustrate a very important principle: I used our children's "rock band" as a teaching moment to help them master the selfishness that I knew was bound up in their hearts. They were intent on pursuing an activity that, although it gave them great pleasure, caused inconvenience and disappointment for many of those around them. And is this not a classic definition of selfishness? They needed to understand that they live in a fallen and broken world, and that part of life in such a world often includes heartbreaking disappointments, crushed emotions and broken spirits. And, incidentally, the musical content of their performance was not altogether for the glory of God—it was more for the glory of self. In the manner that it all played out, this was a much more effective way to learn a valuable life lesson than my simply forbidding them from pursuing their heart's desire. I made a Biblically informed judgment call. In this situation, I did not want to embitter our boys and risk shutting off channels of communication in the future for the greater and more serious lessons in moral decision-making they would have to face.

As parents, we're inclined out of love and a sense of responsibility, to try and meet every one of our children's needs while carefully discerning between needs and wants. We especially and naturally want to protect them from having to face any pain that may come into their lives. However, insulating them from painful experiences now can leave them vulnerable to even more painful experiences in the future if they miss the valuable lessons that ought to be gleaned through unpleasant and difficult trials. Removing them from such testing only encourages more selfishness—that is, "What is in this for me?" Over time, such children would grow to believe—even *insist*—that the world owes them all the license and self-indulgence they desire. In the context of imminent persecution, suffering and self-denial, Peter challenges his spiritual children...

Dear friends, do not be surprised at the painful trial you are suffering, as though something strange were happen-

ing to you. But rejoice that you participate in the suffer-ings of Christ, so that you may be overjoyed when his glory is revealed. If you are insulted because of the name of Christ, you are blessed, for the Spirit of glory and of God rests on you. (1 Peter 4:12-14)

Of course, this is not to say that we should go *looking* for pain, or that we are to intentionally inflict it upon our children. But if they are ever to learn, in Godly humility, that they, as much as we love them, are *not* the center of the universe, we must remain diligent in driving that in-born self-centeredness far from them so that they might see themselves in the context of life's bigger picture—and more importantly, see themselves as God sees them.

If you have more than one child, you have probably discovered that full blown, adult style selfishness begins with self-serving sibling rivalry. Every Saturday morning in our home was the "Mom went shopping yesterday" day. This meant that, on Saturday mornings, the race was on for each of our kids to be the first to get their hands on the one box of the sacred Sugar Smacks cereal. The terrible alterna-tive was the yucky, yet relatively healthy, box of Puffed Rice. If you were not the first on the scene, it was likely you were "Smacks" out of luck.

It didn't take long for one of the brothers to figure out a strategy whereby, not only would he get to the Smacks first, but he could do so and still sleep in. His strategy for "Smacking" down his unsuspecting siblings: simply swap the contents of the two boxes. He knew that none of his sib-lings would dare touch the healthy Puffed Rice box, now filled with the Sugar Smacks. In the foolishness and limited foresight of a child, our son actually thought that his clever strategy would go undiscovered. The guilty son recently reminded me of that tense moment when I uncovered his selfish sin and he watched as I poured myself a bowl of ce-real, expecting Sugar Smacks, but seeing Puffed Rice. This son says he can still see my face when I poured out the substituted cereal. The jig was up, and our son and I shared a wonderful teaching moment together.

The selfishness and rivalry that routinely occurs between brothers and sisters frequently reflects a jealousy that develops when one sibling perceives that another is receiving disproportionate parental attention. You can help curb sibling rivalry by teaching your children early and repeatedly how to honor and respect the rights of others and that property rights are a sacred trust, something that only one or two people—Mom or Dad—can take from them. And, very importantly, you can ensure that you are not unfairly favoring one child over another.

The story of Joseph could lend ample testimony to the trash heap of human devastation caused by parental favoritism (Genesis 37). God ultimately owns all that we and our children possess (Psalm 50:10) and has temporarily consigned them to us as reflections of His goodness. Nevertheless, in our human relationships, the selfish violation of one's property rights—that are so often at the center of family tension—is an offense to God (Exodus 20:15-17).

Solomon tells us in Proverbs 3:27-29...

Do not withhold good from those who deserve it, when it is in your power to act. Do not say to your neighbor, "Come back later; I'll give it tomorrow"—when you now have it with you. Do not plot harm against your neighbor, who lives trustfully near you.

Here, Scripture teaches that God-given blessings should be used as an empowerment to bless others, that we should take advantage of any ability we may have to alleviate another person's pain, and that we should never plot another person's harm in order to gain personally from it. What starts out as swapping Sugar Smacks for Puffed Rice, if left unchecked, could very well lead to a disintegration of moral boundaries that declares, "What is mine is mine and what is yours is also mine."

Observe older siblings carefully when you give them authority over their younger brothers and sisters. Do they use their power to withhold blessings or to generously share? Selfless children grow up to understand that the covenant community begins with the family, that they are called to be God's agents of redemption within their circles of influence, and that all the blessings they enjoy are given for the purpose of becoming blessings to others who are hurting and needy. At all cost, parents must avoid the moral and emotional downward spiral many children experience because of the intended, or even unintended, practice of favoring one child over another.

Pride contributes to emotional bondage.

He [God] mocks proud mockers,
but gives grace to the humble.
Proverbs 3:34

"Lord...Son of David...have mercy on me!" The Canaanite woman's desperate cries were falling on the Savior's seemingly deaf ears, but she was determined to keep trying. *"Have mercy on me, Lord...my daughter is suffering terribly from demon possession!"*

The disciples approached Jesus, annoyed by the woman's persistence. *"Send her away, for she keeps crying out after us!"*

Jesus finally acknowledged the woman's pleas with a rather unexpected answer. *"I was sent only to the lost sheep of Israel...It is not right to take the children's bread and toss it to their dogs."*

"Yes, Lord," the woman replied, as she knelt respectfully before Him, *"but even the dogs eat the crumbs that fall from their masters' table."*

"Woman," Jesus answered, amazed by her response, *"you have great faith! Your request is granted."*

Like this story of the Canaanite woman in Matthew 15:21-28, the Gospel record is full of accounts that portray the virtue of humility—the centurion, for example, who humbly begged Jesus to heal his paralyzed servant (Matthew 8:5-13), or the penitent woman who sorrowfully wiped Jesus' feet with her own hair (Luke 7:37-38). In each instance, Jesus publicly acknowledged their humility as being the central ingredient of great faith.

And, Scripture warns that we must avoid the pride trap...

Do not envy a violent man or choose any of his ways, for the Lord detests a perverse man, but takes the upright into his confidence. The Lord's curse is on the house of the wicked, but he blesses the home of the righteous. He mocks proud mockers, but gives grace to the humble. The wise inherit honor, but fools he holds up to shame. (Proverbs 3:31-34)

Whoever slanders his neighbor in secret, him will I put to silence; whoever has haughty eyes and a proud heart, him will I not endure. (Psalm 101:5)

These warnings are rather hard to miss, aren't they? These are indeed strong words—*violent, perverse, wicked, proud*—and they are the very ingredients that, when mixed together, result in a child becoming a bully. But even stronger words describe how God regards such a person: He *detests, curses,* and *mocks* them. Our children must not envy or admire someone who craves power or takes pleasure in the pain of others. Instead, they should strive to humbly reach out to others who are hurting. Then, God promises to *bless our home, bestow honor,* and take us into *His secret confidence.*

Children must learn that humility is not only the key to greatness, but it is also the channel of God's Grace. The seeds of a growing humility are sown in a child who understands how great a salvation they have been given through Christ, and how great a Mercy has been extended to them through His sacrifice on the cross. Moral failure finds fertile soil in the heart of a child who is gripped by the wrong kind of fear and selfishly learns to pursue only his or her own interests. The only kind of fruit such a child can produce is a proud and stubborn heart. And *God opposes the proud but gives grace to the humble* (1 Peter 5:5). Did you catch that? *God opposes the proud.* This word, *oppose*, means that God treats the proud as His enemy.

We have been looking at ways of guarding our children from pathways to moral failure. The Bible teaches that neither we nor our children are capable of even desiring to live our lives by God's moral principles without our natural hearts of stone being first made into hearts of flesh.

I will give you a new heart and put a new spirit in you; I will remove from you your heart of stone and give you a heart of flesh. And I will put my Spirit in you and move you to follow my decrees and be careful to keep my laws. You will live in the land I gave your forefathers; you will be my people, and I will be your God. (Ezekiel 36:26-27)

You show that you are a letter from Christ, the result of our ministry, written not with ink but with the Spirit of the living God, not on tablets of stone but on tablets of human hearts. (2 Corinthians 3:3)

Only the indwelling of God's Holy Spirit that comes when we place our trust in Christ's finished work on the cross can make all things new and give us and our children a heart's desire to please Him and those around us. Ingraining these principles into our children, and our children's ability to walk in them throughout their lives, is hard work. One might be able to discipline or otherwise persuade their children to become respectful and responsible for a time. They may do so out of fear of or love for you, or simply out of fear of the consequences. But these will prove to be fragile and temporary motives at best. Leading your child to trust in Christ as God's provision for all of their sins and failures and to ultimately desire to please Him is the first step in preparing them for eternity and arming them for the spiritual warfare they will inevitably face throughout life. It also arms them with the proper motive for responsible behavior, namely, the love and fear of God rather than the fear of, or the desire to please, man.

In fact, if you and your children do not have the peace and security in knowing that, when all is said and done, you are completely loved and accepted by God in Christ for eternity, then you certainly will spend the rest of your life on earth trying to fill that void by inflating your own image in the eyes of others and, even if only subconsciously, putting others down so that you may appear to be better. Pride is the sin that transformed Lucifer into Satan. In responding to that beautiful angel's prideful rebellion, God set the precedent for the manner in which He would punish all sin down through the generations of man.

Watch closely for signs that pride may be rearing its ugly head in your children and address it before it becomes an entrenched aspect of their character. If you have missed this one point, most of the contents of this book will be lost on you—namely, that pride is the root of all sin and God hates it, in all its forms.

Undisciplined emotions breed spiritual dropouts destined for moral failure.

Listen, my sons, to a father's instruction; pay attention and gain understanding. I give you sound learning, so do not forsake my teaching. When I was a boy in my father's house, still tender, and an only child of my mother, he taught me and said, "Lay hold of my words with all your heart; keep my commands and you will live."
Proverbs 4:1-4

Our culture needs mothers and fathers who refuse to quit even when they're bruised and discouraged by pain. Spiritual dropouts breed children who will be more likely to become spiritual dropouts themselves. What if our heavenly Father gave up on us? What better motivation than this do you need to never quit on your children? Instead of walking away in disgust from all of us whose hearts are totally depraved, Jesus chose to take upon Himself every one of our burdens, trials and heartaches in a supreme act of love and Mercy—His death on the cross.

Perhaps at this very moment, as you read these words, your heart is breaking because your child has fallen one more time and you're ready to give up on helping him to his personal finish line. Before you lose hope, listen carefully to the *pathos* in the words of this father:

Listen, my son, accept what I say, and the years of your life will be many. I guide you in the way of wisdom and lead you along straight paths. When you walk, your steps will not be hampered; when you run, you will not stumble. Hold on to instruction. Do not let it go; guard it well, for it is your life. (Proverbs 4:10)

Can you hear Solomon's passion as he warns his son not to quit? We will look at the issue of moral failure in more depth when we study Proverbs 5, but for now, don't miss the language used in these verses: *When you walk...when you run...you will not stumble...hold on...do not let go...guard it well.* The slope toward moral failure is a slippery one indeed. And this boy's dad is pleading, above all else, for him not to quit.

It is never too late to turn away from evil and choose righteousness. When your child falls and you sense a spirit of repentance, go back over the process that led to his failure and help him identify each place where he could have made a different choice that would have led to success. You

can start these discussions as soon as your child understands logic, i.e., basic reasoning in how one step leads to
another.

There are three common breeding grounds for moral failure.

Stop listening to instruction, my son,
and you will stray from the words of knowledge.
Proverbs 19:27

He who walks with the wise grows wise,
but a companion of fools suffers harm.
Proverbs 13:20

More often than not, moral failure occurs in children
through one of three environmental influences: **friendships**, **school**, or **dating relationships**.
   ***Friendships are a breeding ground for moral
failure.*** Over the years, there have been far too many
times when I watched parents raise their children on solid
Biblical principles, only to have it all threatened or even
damaged because of the bad chemistry of their relationship
with another child. As parents, we must teach our children
what spiritual "yellow lights" they should look for in relationships—how to spot and avoid a liar, an enticer, or anyone who challenges them to come out from under God-
ordained authority.
   Your children should know how to stand alone when,
through certain relationships or situations, they might
compromise the moral principles with which you raised
them. Once joined with a fool, they will become more foolish. If they make their bed with fools—well, the Scriptures
teach that the companion of fools will be destroyed. The
downward spiral will continue as they then become com-
plicit in the destruction of others.

You should constantly test this chemistry in all your child's friendships, even those with other Christians. Whether a child claims to be a Christian or comes from a Christian home should not be the only measuring stick for whether you allow your own child to develop a friendship with him or her. Remember, foolishness is bound up in the heart of a child, and when the chemistry is not right between two children, trouble will surely follow. When that chemistry is wrong, you must be ready to intervene and cut your child's ties to that unhealthy relationship. You must not be quick to blame the other child for your own child's bad behavior. Instead, look to the dynamic between them. This could go a long way toward preserving your friendship with those other parents.

School is another breeding ground for moral failure. Unless you are homeschooling, your child is in an outside school environment for six or seven hours each day, sitting under the guidance of teachers whom you've probably only met once or twice, if at all. For this reason, you should always be aware of what is going on in your child's school setting. Read through their textbooks and learn everything possible about the instruction they are being given—not only in the classroom, but on the playground as well. Speak diligently with your child about his school experiences. Try to patiently move beyond the evasive response of "OK" when you ask how their day went. Learn how to ask the right questions to unlock their thoughts. Remember, just like their parents, they also need to debrief from a full day.

Depending on your education choice for your child, much of the information being poured into their heads on a daily basis could potentially un-do the Biblical values that you have worked so hard to instill. The blessing and privilege of having found a decent Christian or private school does not relieve parents from their God-given responsibility for monitoring their child's overall education. Sometimes, the flawed or absent moral guidelines that so obviously influence behavior in many public school settings can present just as much of a challenge in the private school setting. What I mean is this—not all Christian parents are raising their children with the same set of values and goals that you're using. And, not all kids who attend such schools have embraced the faith of their parents. Negative peer influence is, at times, just as powerful in the Christian or private school as it is in some of the more questionable public settings. Be very careful to set boundaries specific to your child, with full knowledge of your own child's personality, temptations, and chemistry with other children. Do not easily succumb to your child's plea, "But everyone else is doing it."

Dating is the third breeding ground for moral failure. Dating can be a real nightmare for many parents, especially for dads protecting their daughters as the teen years approach. Although there's much to be said on this topic—enough to fill an entire book by itself—I've summarized what I believe are the important issues and how to address them by laying out some common-sense, Biblically-based principles, or "rules" that I've found to be extremely helpful. Their diligent application will prepare you and your teenager to transform a potential nightmare into a pleasant and rewarding character developing experience. Take the time to study carefully, the **"Ten Common Sense Commandments for Godly Dating"** in the **Teaching Moments** section below.

We've covered much about moral failure in this chapter—what it looks like, how it occurs, and how it can be prevented. At this point, you may be thinking about the principles we've already discussed and the importance of teaching them to your children by the time they're twelve to thirteen years of age. In light of those principles, you may conclude that you're failing, or have failed, in the task of raising Godly children. Always in the forefront of my mind, as I am writing this book, is the family that is dealing with a rebellious teenager or difficult younger child. Parenting done right is the hardest job you will ever have and we are sinners who will make many mistakes in our efforts to raise Godly children. God holds our children responsible for their choices as well as parents who enable them to make the wrong choices.

But, let's take a moment and remind ourselves of the God we serve—the One who's much bigger than any of our weaknesses or failures. Consider once more: *Parenting is not about you.* It's not about what kind of mom or dad you are, but it's about the Grace of God and His Mercy working in and through you. Even though you may make many mistakes, you are not left without hope—because your child *can* be brought back to the foundational principle of learning to fear God, at any stage in life.

Above all else, *never* give up on setting a Godly foundation and example for your children. Even when they may turn away from it, your role as a parent, or even a grandparent, is far from over; you must continue what was already started. May we never give up on raising a generation of children who know, love, and fear God. We can have no higher calling.

Teaching Moments

• The video of Derrick Redmond limping across the finish line of the 400-meter semi-final is not a picture of defeat but a priceless teaching moment on what finishing well in life really looks like. That real quality of character is still recognized and admired by many in our troubled world. Locate a video of Derrick's race on You Tube (www.youtube.com) and watch it with your children. Use Derrick's story to help teach your children that they must finish life's race at all cost, whatever it entails, despite the fact that things may not go quite the way they hoped or expected.

• Teach your young children how to finish well by starting with practical, everyday examples:

o   Expect them to complete all schoolwork and/or household chores.

o   Teach them to stay the course with special projects when the initial excitement wears off and the boredom and the mundane are left to be endured.

o   Teach them the value of working on friendships when conflict arises.

o   Expect them to fulfill their commitments to friends, even when something "better" comes along.

o   Guide them through the chaos of conflict with siblings, no matter how long it takes or how difficult it seems.

o   But the best way to teach your children to stay the course and finish well, is to allow them to see the process through the filtered lens of your own life. That is, you should allow them to see you choosing right when wrong would be easier and initially more beneficial.

•   Look for opportunities in small, daily activities to show your child how the emotions of fear, selfishness, and pride drive their sin. Do not allow them to use these emotions as excuses for bad behavior but rather as a means to help them identify danger signals that will help them choose obedience, and God's blessings that come with obedience, over moral failure.

•   Begin early to teach your child these **Ten Common Sense Commandments of Dating**:

One: This is foundational and requires greater discussion. There are three words in the Greek New Testament that translate into the word "love," but their meanings are very different. Your child's dating relationship must follow a slow developing and ever-maturing pattern, illustrated by these three ever-widening and **concentric circles of mature Biblical love**. The first stage, or inner circle, that forms the core of any God-honoring relationship is the love of God or agape love. It is that soul-spirit love with which God has loved us. It is a love that flows from the cross and forms the spiritual dynamic from which all other forms of love must flow. This love must be the foundation of any good dating relationship. Without it, a couple can never truly enjoy God's best. A young man and a young woman must be first related spiritually as brother and sister in Christ. The clarion call and warning from Scripture could not be clearer:

Do not be yoked together with unbelievers. For what do righteousness and wickedness have in common? Or what fellowship can light have with darkness? (2 Corinthians 6:14)

Have you ever wondered why in that great "love" chapter it says that love is greater than faith or hope?

And now these three remain: faith, hope, and love. But the greatest of these is love. (1 Corinthians 13:13)

The answer may surprise you. You see, when we are in Glory there is no marriage. There is a much greater institution than marriage. Before my wife is my wife, she is my sister in the Lord. There can be no higher relationship between two people. This is why couples who do not share that kind of spiritual intimacy can never truly enjoy God's best. Sure, they can have a "good" marriage as man defines "good," but they can never have God's best so long as that spiritual union is missing. Learning this kind of love starts when your children begin to date. This is the sure foundation.

The next concentric circle of a mature Biblical love is phileos love. This is the emotional, brotherly, or friendship love that flows out of a spiritual relationship. It is this love that builds over time. As their walk with Christ matures, their friendship will deepen into a phileos love. It is this love that characterizes the engagement period, a period that must be lengthy, at least six months to a year, so that the friendship can be truly tested in a variety of circumstances. It is not a reception hall's availability that should determine the length of an engagement, but proper preparation, counseling, conflict resolution and management, and the intense study of God's blueprint for marriage that ought to characterize this sacred period.

The outer concentric circle of a mature Biblical love is eros or sexual love. This love is reserved for marriage and is the fruit of, and the expression of, both agape and phileos love. It is the sexual act inside of marriage that God calls "good." Sexual love (eros) is an act of worship between two people who have discovered agape and phileos love.

In the context of a dating relationship, your child must learn how to move outside of the center of her love—agape love—to see whether a relationship warrants moving ahead with a deeper commitment of phileos love. And when phileos love matures and blossoms into marital love, then and only then may the couple express their sexual love for each other. When this order is reversed, however, the destructive problems that often result can be painful. Human hormones combined with ever-intensifying peer and social pressure result in more and more young people disrupting God's ordained "love sequence."

Two: Your child's dating life must be rooted in a solid, **Biblical worldview** that serves as the grid through which the relationship is evaluated. In other words, your child must have a firm foundational mindset, or she is not ready to date. A Biblical worldview is defined as the foundational core values and beliefs about how and why things happen in the world and how one should respond to them, as viewed from the perspective of the Holy Scriptures.

Three: Both your child and her date must give evidence that they're **under spiritual authority**. That is, you must see evidence that they are committed to the Scriptures, under the authority of their parents, and respectful of all adult spiritual influences God has placed in their lives such as their pastors, teachers, and others.

Four: Dating should be **balanced** with every other area of your child's life so that it doesn't become all-consuming. If she has no interest in other things, or you see that her worldview is being skewed away from the Biblical foundation you worked so hard to build, then she is not ready to date.

Five: Dating should be permitted only after a wealth of experience has proven that your child has a **teachable spirit**. When you begin to see a resistant or argumentative response to your reasonable questions and instructions, then she's not ready to date.

Six: Dating should be permitted in a **group setting**—never alone—during the early stages of a relationship.

Seven: Dating relationships should be **supervised**, even in your own home, to minimize the children's time alone together. Of course, this doesn't mean that you're always sitting directly between your child and her date, but it is important to be aware of what's going on at all times—what they're doing, who they're with, when they're going out, where they are going, and the time *you* set for them to return. You must know about every single detail, and this is a rule that should be strictly enforced, with no exceptions.

Eight: Two-sided **parental communication and involvement** is critical in your child's dating relationship. You must not only get to know your child's date, but also the parents who raised that child, along with their own worldview and value systems.

Nine: Your child should be kept on a **controlled "leash"** of restrictions when it comes to dating. Early on, the leash should be tight and short; then, after your child has earned your trust, the leash can be lengthened. Eventually, after the child has learned how to "heel" and not fight the leash, you won't need a leash at all.

Ten: The relationship should yield a **marked spiritual improvement** in both children in order for it to continue. In other words, if your child and her date are not visibly maturing as Christians, you will know that the dating relationship is wrong.

CHAPTER THREE
The Myth of the Greener Grass

Teach Your Children This Story

KING DAVID HAD a serious problem: his son, Absalom, wanted to kill him. In fact, Absalom was so determined to destroy his father and claim the throne for himself that David was forced to flee for his life.

But David soon discovered that his troubles were about to worsen...

As King David approached Bahurim, a man from the same clan as Saul's family came out from there. His name was Shimei son of Gera, and he cursed as he came out. He pelted David and all the king's officials with stones, though all the troops and the special guard were on David's right and left. As he cursed, Shimei said, "Get out, get out, you man of blood, you scoundrel! The Lord has repaid you for all the blood you shed in the household of Saul, in whose place you have reigned. The Lord has handed the kingdom over to your son Absalom. You have come to ruin because you are a man of blood!" Then Abishai son of Ze-ruiah said to the king, "Why should this dead dog curse my lord the king? Let me go over and cut off his head." (2 Samuel 16:5-9)

Shimei vehemently accused David of something very serious—killing Saul's relatives—that, in fact, David did not do. And to curse the king in this manner was an act that certainly deserved death, just as Abishai was quick to point out.

David, however, had a different response to the situation...

But the king said, "What do you and I have in common, you sons of Zeruiah? If he is cursing because the Lord said to him, 'Curse David,' who can ask, 'Why do you do this?'" David then said to Abishai and all his officials, "My son, who is of my own flesh, is trying to take my life. How much more, then, this Benjamite! Leave him alone; let him curse, for the Lord has told him to. It may be that the Lord will see my distress and repay me with good for the cursing I am receiving today." So David and his men continued along the road while Shimei was going along the hillside opposite him, cursing as he went and throwing stones at him and showering him with dirt. The king and all the people with him arrived at their own destination exhausted. And there he refreshed himself. (2 Samuel 16:10-14)

There's a striking foreshadowing in these passages. We cannot help but notice that, just as King David proceeded along the road while enduring such vicious abuse from Shimei, we see a portrait of the future Son of David—the Savior who would come to save His people from their sins—who would also walk that same road one day on His way to the cross, while willingly enduring the cruel taunting and curses from those who were the very objects of His Grace.

Years later, on his deathbed, David warned another son, Solomon, as he was about to assume the throne...

"And remember, you have with you Shimei son of Gera, the Benjamite from Bahurim, who called down bitter curses on me the day I went to Mahanaim. When he came down to meet me at the Jordan, I swore to him by the Lord: 'I will not put you to death by the sword.' But now, do not consider him innocent. You are a man of wisdom; you will know what to do to him. Bring his gray head down to the grave in blood." (1 Kings 2:8-9)

David's warning to his son was clear: "I did not put Shimei to death, but he is far from innocent. Watch out for this man." The task of dealing with Shimei had now fallen on King Solomon...

Then the king sent for Shimei and said to him, "Build yourself a house in Jerusalem and live there, but do not go anywhere else. The day you leave and cross the Kidron Valley, you can be sure you will die; your blood will be on your own head." Shimei answered the king, "What you say is good. Your servant will do as my lord the king has said." And Shimei stayed in Jerusalem for a long time. (1 Kings 2:36-38)

What a remarkable twist in the story. Instead of justly punishing Shimei for the curses he unleashed on his father, Solomon extended a hand of Grace toward this undeserving man. Although he was forced to live only within the borders that Solomon had established for him, Shimei still received something far greater than he ever would deserve—the king's unmerited favor.

Then, something happened that changed Shimei's fate forever...

But three years later, two of Shimei's slaves ran off to Achish son of Maacah, king of Gath, and Shimei was told, "Your slaves are in Gath." At this, he saddled his donkey and went to Achish at Gath in search of his slaves. So

Shimei went away and brought the slaves back from Gath.

When Solomon was told that Shimei had gone from Jerusalem to Gath and had returned, the king summoned Shimei and said to him, "Did I not make you swear by the Lord and warn you, 'On the day you leave to go anywhere else, you can be sure you will die'? At that time you said to me, 'What you say is good. I will obey.' Why then did you not keep your oath to the Lord and obey the command I gave you?" The king also said to Shimei, "You know in your heart all the wrong you did to my father David. Now the Lord will repay you for your wrongdoing. But King Solomon will be blessed, and David's throne will remain secure before the Lord forever." Then the king gave the order to Benaiah son of Jehoiada, and he went out and struck Shimei down and killed him. The kingdom was now firmly established in Solomon's hands. (1 Kings 2:39-46)

This story demonstrates a principle that's entirely too important to ignore—the principle of moral choice. Shimei was a man who clearly deserved death, and yet was kept alive by King Solomon's sheer grace and mercy. The only catch was that he had to stay within an established set of borders—a sort of house arrest. Otherwise, he was free to live his life as he pleased. The very wise King Solomon was testing Shimei to see if he possessed a heart of gratitude, humility, and obedience after staying his execution. This merciful "gift of life" would have been constantly on the mind of any other grateful and conscientious person under similar circumstances. So why, then, did he step outside of those borders when he knew that doing so would mean certain death?

When Shimei learned of the runaway slaves, he stood in Jerusalem with his eyes fixed on Gath. This is one of the most dangerous postures our children can take—"standing in Jerusalem" with their "eyes fixed on Gath." I can imagine Shimei standing in the streets of Jerusalem, peering longingly into territory that was strictly "off limits," without regard for the consequences of the moral choice he was about to make. He finally went after what he desired in Gath. Solomon, by grace and mercy, had made a covenant with Shimei–stay in Jerusalem or face the consequences. *Shimei abused the grace Solomon extended to him and thus became a covenant breaker.*

Like Shimei, we live every day on borrowed time, deserving death. Yet God, in His infinite Mercy, extends the blessings of His Grace. He extends to us Grace that is common to all men such as food to eat, air to breathe, clothes to wear, water to drink and work to earn a living. This is especially true of life in America. Even His law is an act of Grace, showing us what our King expects of us. And He extends *special Grace* so that all for whom Christ died are enabled to trust Him as their Savior.

Shimei wanted his slaves back since they obeyed his commands and accommodated his every need. Like a child having a temper tantrum, he wanted his way and he wanted it *now*. He would not wait, and he would not be denied. One has to wonder here: who was the true slave? He stood at the crossroads of moral choice, made the wrong one, and it cost him his life. When faced with the choice of embracing or abusing Solomon's grace, Shimei chose the latter, broke the covenant and presumed upon the grace of Solomon. It cost him his life.

Parenting Principle: Presumptuous sin in childhood will lead to the precipice of moral failure in adulthood.

My son, pay attention to what I say;
listen closely to my words.
Do not let them out of your sight,
keep them within your heart;
for they are life to those who find them

and health to a man's whole body.
Above all else, guard your heart,
for it is the wellspring of life.
Put away perversity from your mouth;
keep corrupt talk far from your lips.
Let your eyes look straight ahead,
fix your gaze directly before you.
Make level paths for your feet
and take only ways that are firm.
Do not swerve to the right or the left;
keep your foot from evil.
Proverbs 4:20-27

My son, pay attention to my wisdom,
listen well to my words of insight,
that you may maintain discretion
and your lips may preserve knowledge.
For the lips of an adulteress drip honey,
and her speech is smoother than oil;
but in the end she is bitter as gall, sharp as a double-edged
sword. Her feet go down to death; her steps lead straight
to the grave. She gives no thought to the way of life;
her paths are crooked, but she knows it not.
Proverbs 5:1-6

As a pastor, whenever I have the opportunity to stand
at the altar and perform a marriage ceremony, I will inevitably say these words to the bride, groom, and the entire
congregation that has come together to participate in their
wedding day: "The most important decision you will ever
make is whether you will trust Christ as your Savior and
Lord. After that, there is nothing more important—no job,
no schooling, nothing—than the critical decision about who
you will marry. So, as you stand here today, you are making
that second most important decision." Yet, far too often,
less thought, prayer and preparation go into this life-

changing decision than into our deliberations about where to take our next annual vacation trip!

Disturbing trends in contemporary society reveal little concern for the true human devastation caused by divorce rooted in immorality. Since the introduction of "no-fault" divorce, our country's divorce rate has skyrocketed by over 250 percent. Each year, the statistics grow even more sobering. What's especially troubling is that, before the era of no-fault legislation, back when all the charges and accusations against each other were a matter of court room record, adultery was the number one reason cited as the cause of divorce.

Solomon was a man who was all too familiar with the moral consequences of adultery:

King Solomon, however, loved many foreign women besides Pharaoh's daughter—Moabites, Ammonites, Edomites, Sidonians, and Hittites. They were from nations about which the Lord had told the Israelites, "You must not intermarry with them, because they will surely turn your hearts after their gods." Nevertheless, Solomon held fast to them in love. He had seven hundred wives of royal birth and three hundred concubines, and his wives led him astray. As Solomon grew old, his wives turned his heart after other gods, and his heart was not fully devoted to the Lord his God, as the heart of David his father had been. He followed Ashtoreth the goddess of the Sidonians, and Molech the detestable god of the Ammonites. So Solomon did evil in the eyes of the Lord; he did not follow the Lord completely, as David his father had done. On a hill east of Jerusalem, Solomon built a high place for Chemosh the detestable god of Moab, and for Molech the detestable god of the Ammonites. He did the same for all his foreign wives, who burned incense and offered sacrifices to their gods. (1 Kings 11:1-8)

In these verses, we see the picture of a man who, although considered to be the wisest person on earth, made the kind of moral decisions that ultimately stripped him of his former glory. Ironically, the same king who penned the words of Proverbs 1-9 under the inspiration of the Holy Spirit failed to live up to the very core principles by which he urged others to live.

As we explore King Solomon's life in this context, we must realistically assess our own personal frame of reference by asking and answering the critical questions in this "self-evaluation kit" that will reveal the strengths and vulnerabilities of our own moral fiber:

- Do I, in my own strength, have the power to resist moral failure?
- Have I established adequate moral restraints and borders to help me combat moral temptation?
- Have I realistically considered the destructive consequences of moral failure?
- Do I understand how self-discipline in other areas of my life will help shore up my moral levy?

It is only by the power of the Holy Spirit that we are enabled to resist moral temptation and to erect defensive walls that are impregnable. Only by God's Grace can we recognize that our first inclinations toward adultery are foolish and that there are no exceptions, no matter how sweet and "innocent" the prospect seems. It is through the study of Scripture that we learn Satan's mode of operation, which he employs in those unguarded moments in our day when there is little or no time to reflect on the causes and consequences of our actions.

So, we've gone from the importance of choosing the right life partner in marriage, to the fatal blow that adultery will invariably inflict on a marriage, to the shockingly foolish moral choices of the wisest man who ever lived, to a brief "self-evaluation kit" for inspecting the strength of your own moral fiber. Given the very "grown-up" nature of the moral issues here, it might appear that I've shifted my attention away from our children to addressing only adults. Wrong! One of the best parenting tools is modeling godly behavior for our children.

Every person, young and old, can benefit from this timeless warning issued by the Proverbs 5 father. The very same mortal enemy who breached Solomon's defenses is taking careful aim at our children today. His MO hasn't changed much.

Satan knows where the chinks in your child's armor are to be found.

Unless those weak links are repaired and fortified by the Holy Spirit early in your child's development, Satan will use them as a launching pad for moral failure later. For this reason, it is especially important that you teach your child how to deal with conflicts, as well as other problems or personal weaknesses, in a Biblical manner. Most often, these things are blind spots to your child—i.e., issues others can see that the child himself cannot. When we help our children identify and resolve those issues as they arise, they will be better prepared to resist the assault of the enemy on those chinks in their armor. Though Proverbs 5 specifically addresses moral temptation, these are universal lessons that can train us and our children to humbly identify and acknowledge propensities to specific weaknesses (temptations) and have a plan in place for resisting the call of sin. Your five-year-old will not understand sexual temptation, but perhaps his weakness is coveting what others have. Instead of just forcing him to stop grabbing the belongings of others, this is an opportunity to help him see that discontent might be a root temptation that he will always have to battle. The rules of engagement are the same for all temptation.

Cruelty is another example of a weakness that you may see in your child. If not corrected, it will surface in adulthood in a variety of ways, not the least of which is to hurt someone they claim to love without regard to the pain they're inflicting. Time and again, whenever a man or woman morally falls in their marriage, the rationale is the same: "I deserve to be happy...it doesn't matter that in the process I hurt you. What's most important is *my* happiness." This is selfishness expressed by way of cruelty, plain and simple.

The same applies to a disrespectful attitude or a sharp tongue. If not corrected early, they are likely to sprout up in an ugly way and adversely affect a future marriage relationship. A failed marriage is often rooted in some form of disrespect. Communication breaks down when one spouse verbally abuses the other. Angry, demeaning and hurtful words, once spoken, can't be taken back and cause wounds and scars that never fully heal. These negative behavioral patterns are formed early in childhood.

The chink in the armor could be something that your child is struggling with psychologically or even emotionally. You, as a parent, knowing your child better than anyone, are in the best position to uncover the cause of your child's struggle and deal with it appropriately, seeking spiritually competent help when necessary. But keep in mind that, as your children grow older, Satan will try to use these and other uncorrected weaknesses to lead them into moral failure.

Satan lures our children to fulfill appropriate longings in inappropriate ways.

There are four purposes for the sexual act inside of marriage that God calls "good": to procreate and fill the earth (Genesis 1:28); to leave, cleave, and weave a physical, emotional, and spiritual oneness (Genesis 2:24); to enjoy its pleasures in an unselfish way (1 Corinthians 7:3-4); to illustrate the relationship that Christ has with His Church (Ephesians 5:17-33). But outside these borders, the mental or physical use of sex is defined by God as *adultery* or *fornication*. These are the counterfeits of God's gift and are evil. I used the word "mental" here because the Scriptures clearly warn us that lusting after another in our heart—i.e., mentally picturing a relationship with them—is equivalent to committing adultery (Matthew 5:28).

Children who have no accountability and transparency and who learn early to presume upon the Grace of God or the love of their parents, usually become men and women who have few, if any, moral restraints and pursue certain sin patterns without concern for discovery or consequences. *Teenagers who do not learn to control their appetites never mature and, instead, become men and women who show no submission or accountability to others.* These are the same adults you will find feeding an insatiable lust in front of their computer screens, mesmerized by the enemy who appeals to their base nature and encourages them to fulfill a natural desire in a most unnatural way. When there is no power of the Holy Spirit evidenced in a person's life, there will be no concern over God's disapproval of their actions; that is, they will presume upon the Grace of God without regard for the consequences that will follow the unbridled indulgence of their lusts. They will likely develop a growing dissatisfaction with the affections of their unsuspecting spouse, and the disintegration of the heart of the marriage is not far behind.

Satan is a master at tempting us into presumptuous sin. To avoid Shimei's tragic mistake, we must be careful to never take for granted the Grace that has been extended to us by the King—God's loving Grace that saved us and delivered us into a new and abundant life at a time when we were only deserving of death.

This is one of the most critical lessons we can ever teach our children—*we must never take the Grace of God for granted. We must never presume that forgiveness means there are no consequences to our actions.* Presumptuous sin is one of the greatest ploys Satan will use against your children. Shimei took for granted the incredible act of grace that Solomon had extended to him and, sadly, it resulted in his death. Here was a man who was so thoughtlessly determined to step outside the borders, despite Solomon's warnings, that his determination to pursue his own selfish agenda, above all else, led to his downfall.

The "spirit of Shimei"—or what I prefer to call "presumptuous sin"—exists in every Christian man or woman who makes a conscious decision to morally stray outside God's borders. In this spirit, we *presume* that God is not going to deliver us over to the consequences of our sin—that we're not going to get AIDS or give someone an STD as a result of our immorality. We *presume* that our children will be "fine" despite the fact that their parents are divorcing. We *presume* that God will forgive us—after all, we reason, Christianity is all about love, tolerance, and forgiveness, isn't it? So God will surely keep on forgiving us of our sins, right? This presumptive mindset instills in us a distorted view of the true nature of God, desensitizes us toward sin and leads to the ever more repetitive practice of sin in our lives.

What we so often forget, however, is that, although God is a God of love, He is also a God of justice. This majestic God of love *will* deliver His own children, even ones who have been faithful for years, over to the consequences of those presumptuous sins. Any responsible, loving parent would discipline their child for willful misbehavior. There can be no deeper, longer-lasting demonstration of a parent's love for their child than to seek to drive the foolishness from their hearts—with a strong show of love and reconciliation after the pain of discipline has been experienced.

My son, do not make light of the Lord's discipline, and do not lose heart when He rebukes you, because the Lord disciplines those He loves, and He punishes everyone He accepts as a son. (Hebrews 12: 5-6)

A wise father knows that one of the most effective ways of impressing a truly lasting lesson on a child's heart is to selectively allow that child to experience the "natural cause-and-effect" consequences of his sin. This can often speak louder than a spanking or grounding. God also warns that those consequences will, at His sole discretion, be visited—if not in us, then in our children:

Yet he does not leave the guilty unpunished; he punishes the children and their children for the sin of the fathers to the third and fourth generation. (Exodus 34:7)

Now this doesn't mean that God will not forgive our sins. All of my sins—past, present and future—were paid for at a point in time by His atoning blood. Thus, for the genuine believer, his or her sins have already been forgiven and as redeemed sinners their "vertical" relationship with God is forever established. But God and parents are not obligated to exempt our children from the "horizontal" earthly consequences of their actions. This principle, of course, applies to us as adults as well. Presumptuous sin, or what could be called "the blank-check syndrome," is an offense against God and brings into question the genuineness of one's profession of faith in Christ. If you or your child can comfortably, repeatedly and knowingly thumb your nose at God's Grace, then it is time to search your heart for the likelihood that you are not truly a Christian.

What shall we say, then? Shall we go on sinning so that grace may increase? By no means! We died to sin; how can we live in it any longer? Or don't you know that all of us who were baptized into Christ Jesus were baptized into his death? (Romans 6:1)

Yet, for the genuine believer there is an ongoing process of sanctification that requires constant confession of sin—not in order to restore lost salvation, but in order to restore that open Father-son relationship that we severed when we sinned against Him.

If we confess our sins, he is faithful and just and will forgive us our sins and purify us from all unrighteousness. (1 John 1:9)

In this verse, to "confess" means to "agree with God," that is, to agree to put off the sinful behavior (in this case, the sexual sin) and to put on its opposite and God-like quality (in this case, faithfulness to your spouse and to your God). This two-part process (putting off and putting on) is the very definition of true repentance. It is in this ongoing, daily dynamic with our God that we remain current, and our intimacy with Christ is safeguarded and enjoyed without interruption.

As Christians, we must remember the price that was paid on our behalf in order for God to grant us that forgiveness. We should remember too that the spirit of Shimei lives in every man or woman who claims to love God but is willing to cast aside their families, especially their children and marriages for the sake of their immoral self-indulgence.

Satan lures our children into the wrong crowd so that they will marry the wrong person.

We, including our children, are born under the law and possess a "spirit of Shimei." Just as it was to Shimei, the law has been made clear to us. The Ten Commandments are simple, straightforward, and unambiguous. If we keep all of the commandments all of the time, we will live. Obviously, no one qualifies. Thus, we miss the mark (the definition of sin) and break the law. This brings certain spiritual death. Like Shimei, we are guilty of our crimes and justly deserving the King's displeasure. I can almost hear the angels echoing the words of Abishai as they view the fruit of our hardened hearts: *"Why should this dead dog curse my lord the king? Let me go over and cut off his head"* (2 Samuel 16:9).

We know from firsthand experience that, like us, our children are prone to the spirit of Shimei. Our children are faced with tough decisions every day of their lives. Early in life they will ask and answer some of their own, seemingly innocuous questions: "Should I listen to my mother?" "Should I eat that cookie mommy told me not to eat?" "Should I horde my toys from my nagging sister?" "Should I lie to my daddy?" Their answers to such questions will largely shape their pattern for answering the much tougher questions later on: "Will I trust Christ as my Savior?" "Who will I marry?" "Will I conduct my business with integrity?" "Will I love my wife as Christ loves the Church?" "Will I revere my husband?" "Will I serve Christ as a kingdom-builder?"

The most important decision your child will ever make is to receive God's provision for their sins—the sacrificial death, burial and resurrection of Jesus Christ. On that matter, few, if any, Christian parents would disagree. Now listen carefully. Most of our children will one day face another critical decision that can either lead them to the brook in the way where they will be refreshed daily, or ensnare them in the heat of an arid personal desert of pain and heartache. Like Shimei, they will one day come face to face with a moral crisis of personal choice. Will they leave the presence of the King, step outside of His borders, go whoring after the slaves of lust and marry the wrong person? Will they choose to live a life bound to a partner who is spiritually dead? This is one moral failure that will cost them an abundant life.

I am not suggesting for one moment that a "spiritually-mixed" couple cannot have a "good" marriage. Many do, as the world defines "good." Nor am I saying that a marriage between two believers always translates into a Godly marriage—some matches are living nightmares. What I am saying is this—all that you have done to raise your children to know, love and fear God can be undone in a hormone driven, emotionally charged decision to marry out of lust or expedience rather than out of Godly love. Such a couple can never enjoy God's best for them.

Scripture could not be clearer:

Do not be yoked together with unbelievers. For what do righteousness and wickedness have in common? Or what fellowship can light have with darkness? What harmony is there between Christ and Belial? What does a believer have in common with an unbeliever? What agreement is there between the temple of God and idols? For we are the temple of the living God. As God has said: "I will live with them and walk among them, and I will be their God, and they will be my people. Therefore come out from them and be separate," says the Lord. "Touch no unclean thing, and I will receive you. I will be a Father to you, and you will be my sons and daughters," says the Lord Almighty. (2 Corinthians 6:14-18)

Let's take a look at the imperative verb "do not be" for a moment. When you tell your children "do not" do something, is there any choice left in the matter? When you tell a child not to put his hand in the fire, does that really mean, "Keep your hand out of the fire, but only if you want to"? No, when you tell that child not to touch a hot stove and he chooses to disobey you, what happens? He gets burned!

According to these verses in 2 Corinthians, the same concept, a firm command with no alternatives, applies. *Do not be yoked together with unbelievers* means that under no circumstance are your kids who truly know Christ to marry unbelievers. In fact, I believe this also includes intimate friendships with a non-believer (see Chapter 2 Teaching Moments). Why? The answer is in the rhetorical question Paul goes on to ask: *"What does a believer have in common with an unbeliever?"*

It's a good question and one that deserves careful thought. What *does* a Christian have in common with a non-Christian that would be strong enough to sustain a marriage? Sports, perhaps? Cars? Favorite foods or TV shows? What about the more substantive issues in a marriage? "What are our spending priorities?" "Which group of friends will we hang out with?" "Who is the spiritual leader in the home?" "What church, if any at all, will we attend?" "Which parent will have the biggest say in the spiritual education of our children?" These are areas ripe for deep marital friction and unhappiness.

There are, very simply, two kinds of people in the world—those who are children of God, and those who are not; those who know Christ, and those who do not. The two worldviews are worlds apart! When it boils down to the basic core of our very being and how we will interrelate with someone with whom we will spend the rest of our lives, this question cannot be ignored.

Single Christians who sense in their hearts that "the biological clock is ticking" and that they must marry soon—even if they have to compromise that core-yoking principle in the process—must hold fast to God's promise...

"I will be a Father to you, and you will be my sons and daughters," says the Lord Almighty. (2 Corinthians 6:18)

There is no earthly institution, including a marriage of desperation, which can fulfill us in the same way that God the Father fulfills us as His sons and daughters. Now, I am fully aware that this is a hard truth to live by, especially when desire, romance, or even strong family or social pressure is pulling your heart in a contrary direction. But I must assure you as a pastor that the violation of God's "unequally-yoked" principle has led to more agonizing counseling sessions and marriage break-ups than I can bear to recount. Don't allow your children to go there!

Satan lures our children onto the slippery slope of moral failure.

> *Now then, my sons, listen to me;*
> *do not turn aside from what I say.*
> *Keep to a path far from her,*
> *do not go near the door of her house,*
> *lest you give your best strength to others*
> *and your years to one who is cruel,*
> *lest strangers feast on your wealth*
> *and your toil enrich another man's house.*
> *At the end of your life you will groan,*
> *when your flesh and body are spent.*
> *You will say, "How I hated discipline!*
> *How my heart spurned correction!*
> *I would not obey my teachers*
> *or listen to my instructors.*
> *I have come to the brink of utter ruin*
> *in the midst of the whole assembly."*
> Proverbs 5:7-14

Let these somber words motivate you as a parent to an earnestness and a passion to drive your child far from the precipice of adultery. They warn us of the downward spiral that Satan always takes us on, a spiral that affects every aspect of our lives once we have fallen into the snare of adultery. Follow this progression as we travel with one who has fallen down that slippery slope:

- **He loses honor and strength.**
lest you give your best strength to others... (Verse 9a)

- **He relinquishes control of his future to Satan.**
...and your years to one who is cruel. (Verse 9b)

- **He loses all he has worked toward.**

Lest strangers feast on your wealth and your toil en-
rich another man's house. (Verse 10)

- **His stress affects his body and results in loss**
  of health.
  At the end of your life you will groan, when your flesh
  and body are spent. (Verse 11)

- **He will be tortured by a stinging conscience.**
  You will say, "How I hated discipline! How my heart
  spurned correction! I would not obey my teachers or listen
  to my instructors.... (Verses 12-13)

- **He forfeits covenantal rights and privileges**
  in the Church.
  ...I have come to the brink of utter ruin in the midst of
  the whole assembly." (Verse 14)

In contrast, take a look at the beautiful portrait of
God's blueprint for marriage:

> *Drink water from your own cistern,*
> *running water from your own well.*
> *Should your springs overflow in the streets,*
> *your streams of water in the public squares?*
> *Let them be yours alone,*
> *never to be shared with strangers.*
> *May your fountain be blessed,*
> *and may you rejoice in the wife of your youth.*
> *A loving doe, a graceful deer—*
> *may her breasts satisfy you always,*
> *may you ever be captivated by her love.*
> Proverbs 5:15-19

- **True contentment at home.**
  Drink water from your own cistern, running water
  from your own well. (Verse 15)

- **A Godly influence.**
Should your springs overflow in the streets, your streams of water in the public squares? Let them be yours alone, never to be shared with strangers. (Verses 16-17)

- **Rediscovery of Biblical marital love—one man, one woman, one lifetime.**
May your fountain be blessed, and may you rejoice in the wife of your youth. A loving doe, a graceful deer—may her breasts satisfy you always, may you ever be captivated by her love. (Verses 18-19)

As you're reading this chapter, you may be thinking that you've fallen short of the blueprint for marriage God desires for you—that you have messed up your life and that there is little hope for your kids. You may wonder what good this book could possibly do you now, and what you could possibly teach your children to win them back. But therein is the hope of this book—that imperfect parents throughout history, in faithful reliance upon the instructions and promises of God, have upset the enemy's plans and have raised children who love and serve the Lord. If you will faithfully teach your children the messages of the Proverbs, and if, through your diligence, they lay hold of them in their hearts, God makes you a promise...

I will repay you for the years the locusts have eaten—the great locust and the young locust, the other locusts and the locust swarm—my great army that I sent among you. (Joel 2:25)

He certainly can heal your heart from the wounds of a troubled marriage relationship or even the most painful divorce, and He can mend the damage that your children may have suffered. If this is your circumstance and your heart's desire is for Godly change, I encourage you to make the commitment, establish the necessary borders, and build in the appropriate disciplines for your children to follow. This kind of heart change begins with the fear of God and an absolute trust in His promises. Thus, Solomon returns to the warning he gave us in Proverbs 1:7:

Why be captivated, my son, by an adulteress? Why embrace the bosom of another man's wife? For a man's ways are in full view of the Lord, and he examines all his paths. The evil deeds of a wicked man ensnare him; the cords of his sin hold him fast. He will die for lack of discipline, led astray by his own great folly. (Proverbs 5:20-23)

Teaching Moments

There are some practical things we can do to help safeguard our children from the pitfall of adultery and divorce as they grow older:

• Teach them early that love is more than a mere feeling, but rather a commitment and a discipline in the face of sometimes trying circumstances. They should learn that love requires selflessness and hard work, especially in a marriage, and that love is an act of the will, not just a sentimental emotion.

• Date your children. Start "a date with Daddy or Mommy" when your children are very small. A friend shares how he uses this time to teach his daughters what kind of man he hopes they will marry...

"Being the parents of two girls, it is a seemingly Herculean challenge to teach them about purity, respect for their bodies and standing against the tide of popular opinion which tells young women it's normal to dress provocatively (1 Timothy 4:12 and 1 Thessalonians 4:1-7). As my wife and I pray for our daughters, two themes resound repeatedly: that God would bless them to be leaders, and that, if marriage is part of His plan for them, they will choose husbands who will love, cherish, respect and encourage them. To help shape what they want in a future husband, we started date nights with Daddy. This is a monthly or bi-monthly event in which I take one of our daughters on an evening filled with excitement. The evening usually begins with a movie, then dinner, shopping, things which allow us to sit across from each other and talk—although the shopping thing is quickly becoming an unpopular event for me because of the limited eye contact. I treat them the way I hope men will treat them: I look them in the eye and give them my full attention as we talk, I have a protective spirit as we walk, I open and close the car door for them and I am quick to remind them that when they begin dating that they should expect to be treated similarly by their dates (1 Corinthians 13:1-13). The girls see this as an opportunity to spend more time with Daddy, and that's fine, but I see this as a more focused event in that, as God allows us, I am showing them the chalk lines of dating, boundaries that they will assume when they are out with a young man. These chalk lines allow them to frame-up a mental measuring stick (expectations) which speaks to their comfort in Christ (Hebrews 13:4-5)."

• Teach your children that marriage involves the love of Christ, a love that remains unchanging towards us even when we morally fall. But in order to remain faithful to a spouse, even when they're unloving or unlovable, it is important to maintain a disciplined love for that spouse—the same kind of love that Christ has for us. Model this saying: *The most important thing a father can do for his children is to love their mother.*

• Discourage your children from accentuating outward beauty at the expense of inner beauty. Very young children should not be preoccupied with wearing makeup or faddish clothes, or be so concerned with their outward appearance that they worry about their physical attractiveness to others. Show them the many pictures on the Internet of the so-called "beautiful people" without their makeup. This preoccupation with superficial beauty is a trait that children often see in their parents, so it is important to be a strong role model and keep from sending the wrong signals to your children.

• Teach your saved children to avoid close relationships with non-Christians. Or, if your children have not yet come to faith in Christ, apply this principle anyway, as it will be much easier to win their hearts to Christ if their hearts are not, at the same time, being tempted by the council of the ungodly.

• Teach your children practical steps for fighting temptation. I deal with this more thoroughly in our *Teaching Them Young* study guide (www.markinc.org).

CHAPTER FOUR
How the Mighty are Fallen

Teach Your Children This Story

Persia, around 460 B.C. ...

KING XERXES, RULER of the Persian Empire, called a meeting with his advisors to discuss a very important matter.

His wife, Queen Vashti, had refused to come when the king summoned her into his presence. He was publicly humiliated by her behavior. In Persian culture it was argued that, if this disrespect went unpunished, it would set a dangerous precedent for every other woman in the kingdom to follow. So, the king wondered, what should be done with the queen?

After some discussion, his advisors offered what seemed to be an ideal solution. To ensure that other wives would not be incited to rebel against their husbands, Vashti would be forever banished as the queen of Persia, and the king would begin a search for a new wife to take her place. Pleased with the suggestion, Xerxes sent Vashti away and issued a royal decree ordering that all women throughout the land must respect their husbands.

The king selected his future queen from among the young women, brought from the four corners of the empire, who made up his personal harem. In God's sovereign plan, among the members of the harem was an especially beautiful young girl named Esther. The trusted keeper of the harem was the king's eunuch, Hegai. He was so impressed with Esther's beauty and dignified, respectful behavior that he saw to it that she received favored treatment above all the other women. In fact, he provided Esther with special foods and beauty treatments and moved her and her maids into the most honored position within the harem.

But Esther held a dangerous secret: she was a Jewess who had been orphaned as a child. Her cousin, Mordecai, had raised her and together they belonged to a group of Jewish exiles taken forcefully from the city of Jerusalem. As Esther was growing up, Mordecai gave her strict instructions not to reveal her true nationality or family background to anyone. For years, Esther complied.

In a special God-directed moment, she caught the eye of King Xerxes who saw her as more desirable than any of the other girls in the harem. He had found his future wife. When Esther was crowned the new queen of Persia, the king declared a national holiday and held a special banquet in her honor. The young Jewish girl who had lived her life in quiet obscurity suddenly become a figure of glamour and royalty.

However, all was not well in Persia, as Mordecai would soon discover. While sitting at the king's gate one day, he overheard two officers angrily conspiring to assassinate King Xerxes. Mordecai quickly informed Esther of the plot, and when the report was investigated and found to be true, both officers were hanged. All details of the conspiracy, including Mordecai's discovery of the plot, were recorded in the king's chronicles, although the king himself did not read the account.

Soon afterward, a man named Haman was promoted to the position of the king's chief officer and advisor. Haman's status was higher than that of any of the king's other officials—so high, in fact, that at the king's command, all other royal officers were to kneel before him whenever he passed by. But Mordecai, refusing to engage in such idolatry, never bowed before Haman, despite being repeatedly questioned by the other officers about the matter. Haman was outraged over Mordecai's seemingly irreverent behavior, especially when he discovered that the man was a Jew.

Due in great part to the incredible amounts of wealth and power that his position afforded him, Haman's growing pride and arrogance quickly consumed him. Instead of being content with all that he had, he could only focus on what he perceived to be Mordecai's insubordination. This sent him into a new fit of rage each time the two men crossed paths and Mordecai refused to bow. The thought that someone was so blatantly refusing to pay him homage angered Haman to a boil. Worked up into an arrogant frenzy, Haman devised a plan, under some carefully fabricated pretense, to execute all the Jews in the land, including Mordecai.

With the crafty, morbid details of the scheme beginning to hatch in his mind, Haman approached the king with a suggestion. He said that he knew of a group of people scattered throughout the land, people with foreign customs and beliefs, who refused to subject themselves to the king's laws. If Xerxes issued a royal decree ordering the annihilation of these rebellious people, Haman would offer a financial reward to all the men who swiftly and efficiently carried out the sinister plot.

The king, jealous of his own absolute authority, readily agreed to Haman's proposal, unaware that he was sealing the fate of the entire Jewish population—including his own wife, the queen. And so the decree went out: all Jews, young and old, women and children, were to be executed in a single day...

When Mordecai learned of all that had been done, he tore his clothes, put on sackcloth and ashes, and went out into the city, wailing loudly and bitterly...when Esther's maids and eunuchs came and told her about Mordecai, she was in great distress. She sent clothes for him to put on instead of his sackcloth, but he would not accept them. Then Esther summoned Hathach, one of the king's eunuchs assigned to attend her, and ordered him to find out what was troubling Mordecai and why.

So Hathach went out to Mordecai in the open square of the city in front of the king's gate. Mordecai told him everything that had happened to him, including the exact amount of money Haman had promised to pay into the royal treasury for the destruction of the Jews. He also gave him a copy of the text of the edict for their annihilation, which had been published in Susa, to show to Esther and explain it to her, and he told him to urge her to go into the king's presence to beg for mercy and plead with him for her people.

Hathach went back and reported to Esther what Mordecai had said. Then she instructed him to say to Mordecai, "All the king's officials and the people of the royal provinces know that for any man or woman who approaches the king in the inner court without being summoned the king has but one law: that he be put to death. The only exception to this is for the king to extend the gold scepter to him and spare his life. But thirty days have passed since I was called to go to the king."

When Esther's words were reported to Mordecai, he sent back this answer: "Do not think that because you are in the king's house you alone of all the Jews will escape. For if you remain silent at this time, relief and deliverance for the Jews will arise from another place, but you and your father's family will perish. And who knows but that you have come to royal position for such a time as this?" (Esther 4:1-14)

Esther agreed to go before the king, but urged Mordecai to encourage all Jewish people to fast for three days before she entered the king's presence. Since a holocaust was imminent for all of them, she earnestly sought the support of her people in prayer and fasting before she approached the king to plead for mercy.

On the third day, Esther put on her royal robes and entered the inner palace, in front of the king's hall. Pleased to see her, King Xerxes extended the gold scepter towards her; Esther approached and touched its tip.

Then the king asked, "What is it, Queen Esther? What is your request? Even up to half the kingdom, it will be given you." "If it pleases the king," replied Esther, "let the king, together with Haman, come today to a banquet I have prepared for him." The king immediately ordered that Haman be summoned to attend the banquet, and as the three sat there together, the king asked Esther once again: "What is your request? Up to half of the kingdom, it will be given to you" Esther replied, "My petition and my request is this: If the king regards me with favor and if it pleases the king to grant my petition and fulfill my request, let the king and Haman come tomorrow to the banquet I will prepare for them. Then I will answer the king's question." (Esther 5:3-8)

Haman went home that day in high spirits; he'd been the only guest, besides the king himself, invited to a private party by the queen! He called his wife and friends together that night, taking the opportunity to boast about his vast wealth and all the ways the king had honored him, being sure to point out that the queen had chosen him as the sole guest to attend a very special banquet with the king the next day. But despite his position of influence and power,

Haman had become obsessed with Mordecai, the Jew, sitting each day at the king's gate and repeatedly refusing to kneel before him.

Haman's wife offered a solution: *"Have a gallows built, seventy-five feet high, and ask the king in the morning to have Mordecai hanged on it. Then go with the king to the dinner and be happy." This suggestion delighted Haman, and he had the gallows built* (Esther 5:14).

Determined to carry out his vengeance, Haman was delighted with this suggestion. When morning came, he would have Mordecai executed on the newly built gallows.

That night in the palace, the king's sleep was divinely disturbed. He decided to spend some time reading, so he asked his servants to bring him his chronicles. But as he read through the pages, he was astonished to learn that Mordecai was the one who uncovered the plot to assassinate him, and that he had never been credited or rewarded for it (Esther 6:1-3).

Haman, who had come to speak with the king about his request to hang Mordecai in the morning, arrived in the outer court.

The king said, "Who is in the court?" Now Haman had just entered the outer court of the palace to speak to the king about hanging Mordecai on the gallows he had erected for him. His attendants answered, "Haman is standing in the court." "Bring him in," the king ordered. When Haman entered, the king asked him, "What should be done for the man the king delights to honor?" Now Haman thought to himself, "Who is there that the king would rather honor than me?" (Esther 6:4-6)

The humorous plot thickens.

So he answered the king, "For the man the king delights to honor, have them bring a royal robe the king has worn and a horse the king has ridden, one with a royal crest placed on its head. Then let the robe and horse be entrusted to one of the king's most noble princes. Let them robe the man the king delights to honor, and lead him on the horse through the city streets, proclaiming before him, 'This is what is done for the man the king delights to honor!'" "Go at once," the king commanded Haman. "Get the robe and the horse and do just as you have suggested for Mordecai the Jew, who sits at the king's gate. Do not neglect anything you have recommended." (Esther 6:7-10)

Can you imagine Haman's jaw dropping and his face turning beet-red with rage at this shocking reversal of his plans? But he had his orders. The next day, Haman reluctantly did as the king had commanded. He retrieved the royal robe and led Mordecai through the streets on horseback and then hurried home, covering his head in shame and grief. But the king's eunuchs soon arrived to whisk him away to the queen's banquet, so there wasn't much time to wallow in self-pity. Haman was in an emotional whirlwind and it was very painful (Esther 6:11-14).

As they were both enjoying some wine together at the feast, the king again asked Esther about her request, reminding her that she would be granted anything she desired, up to half of the kingdom (Esther 7:1-2).

"...Grant me my life... and spare my people, for I and my people have been sold for destruction..." Esther finally pleaded. *"If we had merely been sold as... slaves, I would have kept quiet, because no such distress would justify disturbing the king."* King Xerxes asked Queen Esther, *"Who is he? Where is the man who has dared to do such a thing?"* Esther said, *"The adversary and enemy is this vile Haman."* (Esther 7:3-6a)

Suddenly caught up in his own web of deceit, Haman froze in terror before the king and queen (Esther 7:6b). The king stormed furiously out of the room and into the palace garden while Haman stayed behind in the hall to beg the queen for his life (Esther 7:7). But when the king returned from the garden, he found Haman falling all over Esther's couch in pitiful desperation and he exploded in a new fit of rage. *"Will he even attack the queen while she is with me in the house!?"* (Esther 7:8)

"A seventy-five foot high gallows stands near Haman's house," the king's eunuch offered helpfully. *"Haman had it made for Mordecai, who spoke up to help the king"* (Esther 7:9). With one swiftly issued order, the king sealed Haman's fate... *"Hang him on it!"' So they hanged Haman on the gallows he had prepared for Mordecai. Then the king's fury subsided* (Esther 7:9-10).

Oh, how the mighty are fallen!

Parenting Principle: Pride is at the root of all sin.

*To fear the Lord is to hate evil; I hate pride
and arrogance, evil behavior and perverse speech.*
Proverbs 8:13

In Proverbs chapter 6, we read about the Biblical "seven deadly sins." We know, of course, that God hates all sin, but what's so remarkable about these sins in particular? Solomon begins to outline the answer in verses 12-15:

A scoundrel and villain, who goes about with a corrupt mouth, who winks with his eye, signals with his feet and motions with his fingers, who plots evil with deceit in his heart—he always stirs up dissension. Therefore disaster will overtake him in an instant; he will suddenly be destroyed—without remedy. (Proverbs 6:12-15)

Solomon then expands upon this passage in verses 16-19:

There are six things the Lord hates, seven that are detestable to him: haughty eyes, a lying tongue, hands that shed innocent blood, a heart that devises wicked schemes, feet that are quick to rush into evil, a false witness who pours out lies and a man who stirs up dissension among brothers. (Proverbs 6:16-19)

When studying these passages, we should pay special attention to the progressive order of these sins—sins that, if left unchecked, will likely lead to the next sin, and the next...one after the other. The first three on this deadly list are sinful "actions," that is, sins that we can observe, or sins that we can visually see another person *do*. The last four sins on the list speak about the attitudes or conditions of the heart that give birth to those actions. This process of action and thought leads to the total disregard for God's law, denial of the authority of Scripture and, ultimately, to the rejection of Jesus Christ as Lord and Savior. That is why these sins are eternally deadly to the person caught up in them and are an abomination to God.

It is the "haughty" or "proud look" (KJV) that tops this ominous list, since *pride is at the root of all other sin.* Any observant parent knows it is the haughty look that becomes the trademark expression of the child well on his way to rejecting all authority, including God's. The aura of pride is innate in each one of us. In the story of Esther, we read about Haman, whose "haughty eyes" and egotistical pride ultimately led him to the gallows. Haman's life candidly portrayed the flimsy pedestal of pride upon which we love to perch, never realizing that the pedestal's base—our depraved heart—is laced with cracks, as in a glass windshield ready to implode. Pride hinders genuine self-confrontation and hardens us against true repentance. Pride narrows our spiritual depth perception, causing us to focus on pleasing men rather than on pleasing God.

Pride forges an alliance with the foundation of humanism—the worship of man as the ultimate authority in the universe—bound up in each of us. Pride incapacitates us with a spiritual paralysis, preventing us from doing what is right and pleasing to God. It is pride that rejects what is true for what is false and what is right for what is wrong. From the Garden of Eden, the birthplace of secular humanism, it is the Proud One who has never relented in his demonic agenda of redefining the moral standards by which he will live. Humanism is that forbidden tree in the garden where man proudly discerns for himself what is good and what is evil.

God hates pride because it is the root of all other sins. Pride wounds Him, His Church, our families, and our neighbors. Pride is the sin that ultimately leads to all violence and wars, both personal and national. God hates pride because it is the driving force of evil that leads to the rejection of His provision for man's sin, His Son Jesus' death on a cross. Pride fills the quiver of Satan and is the very thermostat that heats the fires of hell where the worm does not die and the thirst of the proud is never quenched. Pride is the sin that has kept millions upon millions of lost souls from receiving the free gift of eternal life.

Consider just a few of the many other verses in Scripture that shows us God's great condemnation of the sin of pride...

Pride goes before destruction, a haughty spirit before a fall. (Proverbs 16:18)

Do not slander a servant to his master, or he will curse you, and you will pay for it. There are those who curse their fathers and do not bless their mothers; those who are pure in their own eyes and yet are not cleansed of their filth; those whose eyes are ever so haughty, whose glances are so disdainful... (Proverbs 30:11-13)

The Lord Almighty has a day in store for all the proud and lofty, for all that is exalted (and they will be humbled)... (Isaiah 2:12)

You save the humble, but you bring low those whose eyes are haughty. (Psalm 18:27)

Pride is embedded in the very nature of our children from the womb. As your children grow, so does their pride. It begins as a mere blemish on his or her spiritual x-ray and slowly becomes a spiritual cancer—a cancer that, if not excised, will eventually invade all of their personality and character. It shows itself with a certain tone of voice, a rolling of the eyes, a contemptuous silence, a cutting judgment, a spirit of premature independence, or an "I-did-not-ask-to-be-born" kind of haughtiness.

Such behavior requires a spiritual biopsy so that you can fully explore its nature. All surgery is painful and uncomfortable. Once excised, this cancer may require even more invasive and painful spiritual therapy. In spiritual terms, an excised sin or sin pattern leaves a vacuum that needs to be filled with something–either Satan will rush in to implant another sin habit, or your Biblically-directed discipline and teaching will ensure that Godly habits and behavior fill the vacuum.

I remember vividly when my wife, Sharon, was diagnosed with stage 3 cancer. We could not see or feel the ominous tumor growing inside of her. But once imaging identified it, we were able to see not only the tumor, but also its ugly, spreading tentacles. Then and only then did we realize how dangerous this really was, how invasive the surgery would be, and how unpleasant and painful would be the treatment she faced. After the trauma of discovery, we faced the harsh reality that, if this was not aggressively treated, she would likely die.

Sensing our fear, the oncologist continuously reminded us that we were going to have to spend the next year of our lives in misery in order to win this war and have the rest of our lives to enjoy the victory. This was not much comfort then. But as we look back, it was what kept us engaged in a positive frame of mind—one year of pain for many years of life. Frequent chemotherapy each month was nasty and debilitating. No sooner would she heal from the monthly treatments and the horrible side effects than it would be time to re-enter the hospital to do it all over again. But we kept the goal in sight—a cancer-free woman who would live to be a mother to her kids, a wife to her husband, and a grandmother to her not-yet-born 14 grandchildren. The goal became everything.

This is how you must deal with pride in your child—it is an ugly tumor that must be excised. It is a war, a war of relatively short-term pain with long-term healing. Frequent treatments will be required with heavy doses of spiritual-therapy over the many years God entrusts them to your care. These battles will not be pretty and the patient may sometimes resist. Yet, you must keep your eye on the goal—raising a humble man or woman who is a channel of God's Grace. This is why we need to lead them to take a long, hard look at the examples God has given us in His Word, such as we find in the Book of Esther or in these verses from James 4:

What causes fights and quarrels among you? Don't they come from your desires that battle within you? You want something but don't get it. You kill and covet, but you cannot have what you want. You quarrel and fight. You do not have, because you do not ask God. When you ask, you do not receive, because you ask with wrong motives, that you may spend what you get on your pleasures. You adulterous people, don't you know that friendship with the world is hatred toward God? Anyone who chooses to be a friend of the world becomes an enemy of God. Or do you think Scripture says without reason that the spirit he caused to live in us envies intensely? But he gives us more grace. That is why Scripture says: "God opposes the proud but gives grace to the humble." (James 4:1-10)

Did you catch that last phrase? God *opposes the proud.* This literally means that God *treats the proud as an enemy.* And there is nothing more terrible to contemplate than the prospect of being branded by God as His enemy. It would be a dark sentence of abject hopelessness, given the geyser of poisonous pride that gurgles beneath the surface in all of us, if the verse ended there. But verse 10 goes on to say that God also *gives grace to the humble.* As parents, we must diligently teach our children that *humility is the key to greatness and the conduit of God's Grace.* As God gives you more Grace to teach humility to your kids, their humility becomes the conduit of true spiritual power in their lives. They must learn that no one's pride—including their own—is so deep and so cancerous that God can't excise it. This is why you do well to teach them this wonderful story of Esther and Haman while they are very young. Through it, they will learn that God certainly knows how to humble us in a variety of unexpected ways.

The Sermon on the Mount is the New Testament Constitution. In that series of homilies, Jesus declares the Kingdom-mandate for His Church. The Beatitudes are the preamble to this Constitution, where He lays out for us and our children the character of soul He expects of the citizens in His kingdom. How and where does Jesus begin? He begins in the same place Solomon did in his discussion of the seven deadly sins—with the sin of pride. *"Blessed are the poor in spirit, for theirs is the kingdom of heaven"* (Matthew 5:3).

One who is *poor in spirit* is a truly humble person, someone who understands that humility is the channel of God's Grace. If our children are to become poor in spirit, if we are to teach them the humility and the Grace of God, then we must first take our own spiritual CAT scan and hold it up to the light of Scripture so that we might see our own tumors of pride. Then and only then do we have the moral prerogative to take our child's spiritual scan and begin the hard work of surgical excision. And as God humbles us, we will be more empowered to deal with the evil root of pride by way of the painful, and often ugly, spiritual therapy that will insure long-term healing. In the next chapter, we will take a close look at the other "deadly sins"...

Teaching Moments

• One of the best ways to break the sin of pride in your kids is by practicing humility yourself. Do your children ever see you admit your own wrongs to others and seek their forgiveness?

• Are you willing to admit when you have wronged your kids, and seek their forgiveness? It is not enough to say that you are sorry. Sorrow is a passive humility. You must also ask, "Will you forgive me?" This is an active humility, requiring a response on the part of the other person.

• What do your kids observe in your interactions with the authorities in your life such as your spouse, your church leaders, your boss, or your political leaders? Are you demonstrating true humility?

• Do you see the discipline of your kids through to a good conclusion, or do you give up on the hard work of discipline when genuine repentance is a long time coming? Humility does not come without true repentance, and true repentance does not come without two-factored change. That is, the ungodly behavior must be put off and its opposite Godly quality must be put on. Study with your kids Ephesians 4:25-32. Note the two-factored change process Paul speaks of in this passage:

Therefore each of you must put off falsehood and speak truthfully to his neighbor, for we are all members of one body. In your anger do not sin: Do not let the sun go down while you are still angry, and do not give the devil a foot-

hold. He who has been stealing must steal no longer, but must work, doing something useful with his own hands, that he may have something to share with those in need. Do not let any unwholesome talk come out of your mouths, but only what is helpful for building others up according to their needs, that it may benefit those who listen. And do not grieve the Holy Spirit of God, with whom you were sealed for the day of redemption. Get rid of all bitterness, rage and anger, brawling and slander, along with every form of malice. Be kind and compassionate to one another, forgiving each other, just as in Christ God forgave you.

CHAPTER FIVE
Is Your Child a Darth Vader?

Teach Your Children These Stories

OUR KIDS' FIRST exposure to the movie *Star Wars* quickly captured our son, Dan's, imagination, and from that moment his long-term love affair with all things *Star Wars* was launched. Now his children love waving their own light sabers and learning life lessons from the adventures of Luke Skywalker and Darth Vader.

The arts, Christian or secular, are chock-full of parental teaching moments and, with careful screening, you can help shape your child's worldview by plugging into the power of popular movies. Mention Darth Vader to children of the 70's and 80's, and their children, and they immediately remember his classic challenge to his son, "Luke, come over to The Dark Side." As portrayed in all *Star Wars*-related media, The Dark Side represents pure evil drawn from such emotions as fear, rage and hatred. In prequel films, The Dark Side draws its power from all strong emotions when fueled by jealousy, possessiveness, and fear of loss.

Speaking of The Dark Side, meet Gehazi (2 Kings, Chapter 5), one of the most privileged young men of his day. God's prophet, Elisha, was his mentor and was groom-

ing Gehazi to lead a fledgling class of "seminary students"—
until one fateful day, when Naaman, the Syrian, came to
pay a visit. Who would have thought that this seemingly
Godly young man could so easily step over to The Dark
Side?

Naaman was the successful and wealthy commander of
the great Syrian army. But all of that faded into insignifi-
cance when he began to notice painful patches of skin de-
formities appear all over his body. Leprosy! Naaman knew
he would die a slow, horrible death from this dreaded disease and he was desperate to find help. Naaman heard a
rumor about a man who had mysterious healing powers, so
with the Syrian king's permission, and a sack full of gold
and silver in hand, he set out on a journey to find Israel's
prophet Elisha.

If you knew that the President's chief representative
was coming to your house, how would you get ready for his
arrival? Do you think you might be a little bit nervous?
Word got to Elisha about his approaching guest, but this
prophet of God didn't bother to even come out and greet
him! Instead, as Naaman pulled his chariot up to the front
of the prophet's house, Elisha sent a servant out to give him
some rather unusual instructions: *"Go, wash yourself sev-
en times in the Jordan, and your flesh will be restored and
you will be cleansed"* (2 Kings 5:10).

What? Naaman was furious and humiliated! Take sev-
en baths in the river? *That* was the great healer's remedy?
Given his high political stature and the fact that he had
traveled so very far, why did this man Elisha not even
bother to meet him personally? And who was this insignifi-
cant lackey he'd sent as a messenger instead? Didn't he deserve more respect than that? At the very least, Naaman
thought that the healer would come outside, call on the
name of his God in an appropriately dignified ceremony,
wave "magical" hands over his leprosy, and cause his white
decaying skin to become perfectly healthy. Furthermore,
why should he bother to wash in the Jordan River, of all

places? Weren't there other bodies of water closer to home that were more suitable for royalty's guardian?

But his servants, perhaps weary from travel or at least intrigued by the strange spectacle, offered their commander some sage advice: *"My father, if the prophet had told you to do some great thing, would you not have done it? How much more, then, when he tells you, 'Wash and be cleansed!'"* (2 Kings 5:13)

Naaman finally relented, went down to the Jordan River, and dipped himself in the water seven times. As he came out of the water, his skin was suddenly restored to normal. The leprosy was gone! Naaman was ecstatic!

Naaman returned to Elisha, a changed man and anxious to express his gratitude: *"Now I know,"* he said, *"that there is no other God in all the world except in Israel. Please, accept a gift from your servant"* (2 Kings 5:15).

But in spite of Naaman's urging, Elisha refused to take anything from the warrior.

"As surely as the Lord lives, whom I serve, I will not accept a thing." "If you will not," said Naaman, *"please let me, your servant, be given as much earth as a pair of mules can carry, for your servant will never again make burnt offerings and sacrifices to any other god but the Lord. But may the Lord forgive your servant for this one thing: When my master enters the temple of Rimmon to bow down and he is leaning on my arm and I bow there also--when I bow down in the temple of Rimmon, may the Lord forgive your servant for this."* (2 Kings 5:16-18)

Naaman already showed the first indication that he was moving away from The Dark Side into the light of God's love. He knew he could not worship anyone but the One True God. *"Go in peace," Elisha said* (2 Kings 5:19).

Gehazi watched silently as Naaman and his servants departed. Surely, he thought, the great prophet was beginning to show signs of senility. Elisha—his mentor, master, and spiritual leader—had been far too dismissive of the generous cash offer. Naaman was obviously very wealthy. Why did Elisha refuse his gift of money and goods in exchange for the healing of his leprosy? There were so many worthy causes for which they could have used that money in their emerging and yet-fledgling seminary!

Taking matters into his own hands, Gehazi hurried after Naaman's chariot and breathlessly caught up with the entourage.

"Is everything all right?" Naaman asked, stopping the chariot when he noticed Gehazi running behind him. "Everything is all right," Gehazi answered. "My master sent me to say, 'Two young men from the company of the prophets have just come to me from the hill country of Ephraim. Please give them a talent of silver and two sets of clothing.'" "By all means, take two talents," said Naaman. He urged Gehazi to accept them, and then tied up the two talents of silver in two bags, with two sets of clothing. He gave them to two of his servants, and they carried them ahead of Gehazi. (2 Kings 5:21-23)

When he approached his house, Gehazi took the items from the servants and hid them inside, in his own strong box, before returning to Elisha.

"Where have you been, Gehazi?" Elisha asked (2 Kings 5:25a).

Uh oh, Gehazi must have thought. This was his opportunity to tell his master the truth. It wasn't too late to repent of his presumptuousness and deception, but Gehazi had already made his choice to wallow on The Dark Side.

"Your servant didn't go anywhere," Gehazi answered (2 Kings 5:25b). Surely he didn't say that, did he?

Gehazi's own words condemned him. God had already revealed to Elisha that his protégé was lying. *"Wasn't my spirit with you," he said, "when Naaman got down from his chariot to meet you? Is this the time to take money, or to accept clothes, olive groves, vineyards, flocks, herds, or menservants and maidservants? Now Naaman's leprosy will cling to you and to your descendants forever"* (2 Kings 5:26-27).

Gehazi's sin was that he lied against the Holy Spirit when he lied against God's prophet. Gehazi left Elisha's presence, and with each step his entire body grew whiter and whiter with the loathsome and dreaded disease. The lie he'd told had not only seemed relatively harmless, but he truly believed that he'd had good reason for telling it. What wouldn't he give to undo the last hour of his pitiful life! But, sadly, it was too late—Gehazi would have to live with the consequences of his lie for the rest of his life...

Ananias and Sapphira: A doomed couple

Now, let's fast forward a few centuries to around A.D. 35 and meet a married couple who failed to heed the lessons of Gehazi—lessons they had likely been taught from Sabbath school to adulthood. They followed in Gehazi's footsteps over to The Dark Side and paid with their lives.

Imagine that you are in a foreign country, standing in a courtyard with thousands of people from all over the world. You are listening to a preacher, but you can't understand his words because he's speaking in another language. Suddenly, bright flames of fire land on top of each person's head and people who had never taken a single foreign language class start talking in other tongues! An Ethiopian turns to your family and interprets the words of the preacher in your own language. People from all over the world are hearing about Jesus for the first time in their own language!

This actually happened right after the resurrection of God's Son, Jesus Christ. Language barriers were broken down so that the Good News could be preached and understood. Thousands of people were brought to faith in Christ with just one preached message from the lips of the disciple, Peter, who had only recently acted with cowardly denial toward his Lord. This miracle produced a renewed hope in a people who had been mired in virtual slavery. Could their long-awaited Messiah have finally come? Could this Jesus be the one who would miraculously deliver them from the evil power of Rome?

The young church grew quickly, but coming to Christ was risky. Oppression by the Jewish leaders was so severe that it was virtually impossible for any Christian to secure a job. Since all of the trade unions were controlled by the enemies of "The Way," the jobless numbers among the believers was high. They could not earn enough money to support themselves and their families. To help meet the needs of this first century "recession," especially among the widows and orphans, the Christian community pooled their resources and created a deacon's fund that was regularly distributed according to need. The wealthier church members who could afford to do so regularly sold off some of their assets, such as land, and contributed the proceeds to the fund.

Ananias and his wife, Sapphira, were among the wealthy believers who chose to sell some of the property that they owned. This was commendable at first glance, but The Dark Side quickly beckoned to the couple.

Ananias and Sapphira sold their land and declared that they were giving the entire sale price to the deacon's fund. But this was a lie. Their real plan was to secretly keep a portion of the proceeds for themselves and deceive the church into believing that their gift was more sacrificial than it really was. "This is so much money, surely there is no harm in keeping some of it for our own financial security," they reasoned. After all, the church should be grateful for their generosity.

But God knew their hearts, and told the Apostle Peter. In Elisha-like fashion, Peter confronted Ananias as soon as the money was laid at his feet...

Then Peter said, "Ananias, how is it that Satan has so filled your heart that you have lied to the Holy Spirit and have kept for yourself some of the money you received for the land? Didn't it belong to you before it was sold? And after it was sold, wasn't the money at your disposal? What made you think of doing such a thing? You have not lied to men but to God." (Acts 5:3-4)

Immediately, Ananias dropped dead! The ushers came forward, took his body out, and prepared it for burial.

Sapphira appeared several hours later.

Peter asked her, "Tell me, is this the price you and Ananias got for the land?" "Yes," she said, "that is the price." Peter said to her, "How could you agree to test the Spirit of the Lord? Look! The feet of the men who buried your husband are at the door, and they will carry you out also." At that moment she fell down at his feet and died. Then the young men came in and, finding her dead, carried her out and buried her beside her husband. Great fear seized the whole church and all who heard about these events. (Acts 5:8-11)

Just like Gehazi had an opportunity to repent and tell the truth, God gave Sapphira the same opportunity—but she, too, chose The Dark Side.

Parenting Principle: Your child has an innate tendency toward The Dark Side.

*There are six things the Lord hates,
seven that are detestable to him:
haughty eyes, a lying tongue, hands that
shed innocent blood, a heart that devises
wicked schemes, feet that are quick to rush
into evil, a false witness who pours out lies
and a man who stirs up dissension among brothers.*
Proverbs 6:16-19

Genocide in Darfur...terrorists' murderous rampages...AIDS, famines, drug addiction, political corruption, and world wars. We can readily agree that these things are the rotten fruits of mankind's dark side. What else can explain a band of thugs high-jacking a bus in Afghanistan and killing all forty-four people on board, beheading many of them, including women and little children? Such is the depth of human depravity and our abject inability, within our own resources, to control it. And without a Biblical understanding of the innate sinfulness of man, we would have absolutely no explanation as to why these rotten fruits and mindless depravities even exist.

As we already discussed in the last chapter, the seven "deadly" sins of Proverbs 6:16-19 are the structural framework of evil that exists in each and every one of us. Flowing from the sin of pride is a progression of evil that over time grows like a wild tumor in intensity. Put another way, few of us realize the depth of evil to which we are capable of sinking if the right circumstances presented themselves.

As parents, we must remember that the spirits of Gehazi, Ananias and Sapphira, live in our children as well. In fact, every one of us starts out on The Dark Side, symbolized by the character of Darth Vader. We are sinful enemies of God from the moment of conception because we are children of Adam. When God blesses us with children, we contract for a lifetime of teaching them that God detests evil, that there are Gehazi-like consequences that always result from sin, and that the wages of sin is always death. Solomon warned his young son in Proverbs 6 of the things God hates. God *hates* sin.

Consider what transpired on the cross. There on that little mountain shaped like a skull, God the Father turned His back on God the Son, refusing to look upon Him even amidst the screams of *"My God, My God, why have you forsaken me?"* Why? Because, at that moment, Jesus bore in His own body the sins of His people, and a Holy God will not look upon sin. This is the "battle cry" that our children must sound when tempted by the enemy of their soul, the Darth Vader within. The proud look or the haughty eyes, if left unchecked, continues with a deadly progression.

A Lying Tongue

The Lord detests lying lips,
but he delights in men who are truthful.
Proverbs 12:22

In the stories of Gehazi, Ananias, and Sapphira, at first glance, one might wish to argue that the lies did not warrant leprosy and death. Can't our loving, understanding God look the other way if I just tell a well-meaning "white lie" now and then? But consider the company a liar keeps...

But the cowardly, the unbelieving, the vile, the murderers, the sexually immoral, those who practice magic arts, the idolaters and all liars—their place will be in the fiery lake of burning sulfur. This is the second death. (Revelation 21:8)

Did you catch that? God has expressly included *all liars* among those who will have a place in the fiery lake of burning sulfur. Certainly, this list of offenses implies a lifestyle of egregious behavior where injury to another is habitual. One can argue that the "little white lies," like when your child steals a cookie but tells you he didn't, rarely produce such injury. But like all sin, lying is habit forming. What is allowed in moderation will be excused in excess. Our children must put off the sin of lying and put on the habit of truth-telling. The unrepentant "white lies" liar will become the Darth Vader of liars who is in danger of hellfire.

The authority of the Prophets and the Apostles is clear—they are the twenty-four elders who encircle the throne of Grace in heaven (Revelation 4:4). In both stories, the lies were told to God-ordained authorities. Thus, when Gehazi lied, he lied not only *to* the prophet Elisha, but also *against* the Holy Spirit who had anointed Elisha to that office. And when Ananias and Sapphira lied, they lied not only *to* the Apostle Peter but also *against* the Holy Spirit who had anointed Peter into that office—thus, the gravity of their sin. All lies are not merely directed against another human being, but against God Himself. He takes it personally when we lie!

Some of us rightly believe, as theists do, that God knows where we've been, what we've done, what we think— and yes, when we lie. But then we live as practical deists, believing our God is detached from our human experience. Yet, He is anything but detached: *"O Lord, you have searched me and you know me. You know when I sit and when rise; you perceive my thoughts from afar. You discern my going out and my lying down; you are familiar with all my ways"* (Psalm 139:1-3).

The eyes of the Lord are everywhere, keeping watch on the wicked and the good. (Proverbs 15:3)

God hates lying because it is contrary to His nature as the God of all Truth. Lying breaks down the foundation of a man's character, for no one can trust a liar. Lying disintegrates family trust and destroys channels of communication. Our culture is steeped in lies, from commercials promising the fountain of youth to millions of pornography sites that promise to satisfy our sexual needs, to politicians who promise to solve all of society's ills in return for your vote. It is from the fountain head of lies that racism, deviant sexual behavior, and injustice flow. Slavery was rooted in the lie held by many, including people who claimed to know Christ, that some men were to be considered less-than-human, mere property to be bought and sold, simply because of their skin color. It is from the father of lies, Satan himself, that babies are scraped, sucked, and burned from the womb. Lies sent the Son of God to an ignoble death on the cross.

From the very beginning, the enemy has been distorting God's words with half-truths in keeping with his vocation as the father of lies (John 8:44). Through a clever web of lies, Satan has convinced millions of unsuspecting souls to believe that all religions are equally valid pathways to God, or that hell is merely a place where "bad" people will go to enjoy drunken orgies with their friends. Satan's deception leads us to believe that, if we drug up, drink up, inhale, or indulge in illicit sex often enough, then peace and lasting contentment will come as the result.

Satan, the liar that he is, convinces us not to share our Christian faith with others, even when the door of opportunity is wide open, since religion is a *personal* matter. And to the seeker, he whispers that the Church is filled with hypocrites, or has failed them if all of their personal longings for happiness are not being met. The most tragic of all of Satan's lies is that a sufficient list of good works, performed with deep sincerity, will counter-balance the sin in our lives and "buy" us salvation.

No matter in what form the sin of lying is packaged—whether it's outright untruths, half-truths, innuendo, exaggeration, or even the avoidance of guilt by putting on a façade of innocence—we must teach our children that *God detests lying lips, but he delights in men who are truthful.* (Proverbs 12:22). The capability to become a recalcitrant liar is inherent in all of us. Our children must learn early the importance of always telling the truth, even if that truth is difficult—because it is far better to speak the truth in love than to become that which is detestable to God.

Hands That Shed Innocent Blood

> *There are six things the Lord hates,*
> *seven that are detestable to him:*
> *haughty eyes, a lying tongue,*

hands that shed innocent blood...
Proverbs 6:16-17

The greatest of all sins ever committed by mankind is the rejection of Jesus Christ as the Savior of the world. This is the epitome of the shedding of truly innocent blood. Note the progression of the deadly sins in the following–the *pride* of Herod, the Sanhedrin, and Pontius Pilate, leading to a mockery of justice loosely called a trial, with *false witnesses* (liars) to convict Him and shed His *innocent blood*.

Satan's ultimate objective throughout history has been to capitalize on our pride in order to generate lies and confusion about the identity of Christ and His offer of salvation. It is pride that is at the heart of one's rejection of Christ. Pride gives birth to lies and lies give birth to doubt; doubt and unbelief lead to the rejection of the truths of Scripture and the claims of Christ.

Since he can't actually take away our eternal salvation, Satan's desire is to do the next best thing: to create false doubt in our minds and hearts about the veracity of our salvation. Just as it is with half-truths that the Evil One tempted Jesus, it is with half-truths that he desires to rob us of the assurance of our salvation. Our kids will be tested by many doubts and fears, but remember that all lies are designed to lead us toward *the rejection of Christ Himself.*

When we look to anything other than the cross of Christ for a solution to our depraved condition, we are blinded as to what our sin actually cost Him. We refuse to see that it was our inherent pride that beat Him to a bloody pulp, our lies that spat on Him, our maliciousness that mocked Him, our love of this fallen world that stripped Him naked, and our selfishness that hammered the nails, blow by painful blow, into His hands and feet. Our rejection of so great a salvation is the sin that effectually thrust a spear into His lifeless side, and that buried Him in a cold tomb. And there, but for Grace, all mankind would be hopelessly hell-bound for a Godless eternity. But incredibly, in spite of it all, Christ's love reaches out to our children—with resurrection power, with everlasting Mercy, with peace that surpasses all understanding, and with an unspeakable joy.

It is in the progression of the first three of these deadly sins that our vertical relationship to God spirals downward; it is in the progression of the last four of these deadly sins that our horizontal relationships and friendships cast us headlong into devastating and destructive quicksand.

The Bitterness of Unresolved Conflict

> *...a heart that devises wicked schemes,*
> *feet that are quick to rush into evil,*
> *a false witness who pours out lies and a man*
> *who stirs up dissension among brothers.*
> Proverbs 6:18-19

Trouble was brewing in the church at Philippi. In many respects, the body of believers at Philippi were a model church—in fact, the Apostle Paul openly proclaimed his thankfulness to God for every time he thought about the Christians in Philippi (Philippians 1:3). But in the midst of a letter filled with warm greetings and exhortations, he also issued an urgent plea to two important women of the church...

I plead with Euodia and I plead with Syntyche to agree with each other in the Lord. Yes, and I ask you, loyal yoke-fellow, help these women who have contended at my side in the cause of the gospel, along with Clement and the rest of my fellow workers, whose names are in the book of life. (Philippians 4:2-3)

Although just two verses in the book of Philippians hint at an apparent disagreement between these women, it was a matter that Paul felt deserved the attention of the entire congregation. Euodia and Syntyche were believers.

Paul says that their names were written in the Book of Life. They contended at Paul's side for the Gospel at great personal cost. They were indwelt by the same Holy Spirit, and they stood shoulder to shoulder as prayer warriors and soul winners—likely hosting a house church together. But something troubling happened between these two champions of the faith—some strong, interpersonal conflict that caused a rift deep enough for Paul to intervene in the crisis and encourage the counseling of the church "yokefellow" or mediator. We are not told the exact nature of the disagreement, but as is usually the case with these rifts, the healing was more critical than the details of the disagreement.

Unresolved conflict, as with all sin, is mired in pride. As one of the seven deadly sins, unresolved conflict can be severely damaging if it is not handled in a Biblical manner. What can start out as a disagreement between a brother and sister, or a parent and a child, can eventually lead to a bitterness of the soul. Bitterness defiles, is a cancer to the soul, and robs us of peace with God and man.

We all know of ongoing personal conflicts in our circles of influence. Some lead to silent treatments that go on for years, while the original cause of the conflict may be long forgotten. Tragically, the treasures in our short lives that could have been shared are lost forever—and Satan rejoices. All who know Christ have His Holy Spirit and are commanded to not let unresolved conflict simmer (Hebrews 12:14-15). With that Holy Spirit we also have the power to take that first step of grace, to be the first one in the standoff to "blink," and take all necessary steps to work out the differences peaceably and in humility. Because pride and pettiness rob us of abundant life (John 10:10), we must bring our conflicts and bitterness to the foot of the cross.

It may be necessary to "agree to disagree" so that we can live at peace with all men. Our children grow up in our homes and they are watching how we handle conflict. When they marry, they will likely follow your pattern. Remember, humility is the key to greatness and God hates pride. Can it be any clearer than this...?

Make every effort to live in peace with all men and to be Holy; without holiness no one will see the Lord. See to it that no one misses the grace of God and that no bitter root grows up to cause trouble and defile many. (Hebrews 12:14-15)

Satan purposes to stir up dissension—conflict rooted in pride that divides the family, the races, the sexes, the Church, and the nation. Out of the depravity of our hearts, conflict usually emerges because of idol worship. Can you see rudiments of the following idols in your kids?

• **The idol of power.** Conflict arises in the pursuit of control—controlling how other people act or feel about you, or vice versa—in an insatiable lust for power.

• **The idol of jealousy.** Coveting what another person has—a jealous spirit that causes us to look for ways to discredit the person who has what we do not have. Our victim must be demeaned so that we may feel better about ourselves in the destructive process.

• **The idol of obsession.** Many of us live our lives—especially in our marriages—obsessed with always being right. We do not look for I win-you win outcomes; instead, we look for *I win-you lose* outcomes.

• **The idol of rebellion.** Rebellion against the spiritual authority structures in your life, such as marriage, church, job, and even government, serves as a potential springboard for conflict. As your children observe this spirit in you, they will unquestionably develop the same attitude themselves.

Power grabbing, coveting, jealousy, obsession, and rebellion, if left unchecked, *will* come out eventually, like an adder's poison spewing from the depth of our soul. The seeds of conflict are sown by unhappy people with "unhappy feet" that are quick to spread trouble and desperate to find comrades and sympathizers in their misery. They must keep the flow of dissension alive and infect others with their discontent and unhappiness. They refuse to do the hard work of resolving those conflicts. Consider the following verses...

Woe to those who plan iniquity, to those who plot evil on their beds! At morning's light they carry it out because it is in their power to do it. (Micah 2:1)

Their feet rush into sin; they are swift to shed innocent blood. Their thoughts are evil thoughts; ruin and destruction mark their ways. (Isaiah 57:9)

Their throats are open graves; their tongues practice deceit. The poison of vipers is on their lips. Their mouths are full of cursing and bitterness. Their feet are swift to shed blood; ruin and misery mark their ways, and the way of peace they do not know. There is no fear of God before their eyes. (Romans 3:13-18)

Did you catch that last sentence? *There is no fear of God before their eyes.* There it is again: the fear of God is the beginning of Wisdom. Destructive schemes and plots come from people who do not fear God. Like Euodia and Syntyche, many Christians get so caught up in fighting and bickering with each other that they forget who the real enemy is. They lay awake at night tossing and turning, plotting how to get even when, instead, they should be losing sleep over the millions of souls that are on their way to hell. And when a brother or sister is wounded, we do not apply the balm of healing. Instead, many in the Church have acquired the unsavory knack of shooting our wounded.

Instead of advising the quarreling women that they were incompatible with each other, or that the problem between them had existed too long for any real healing to take place, the Apostle Paul offers them hope—and a challenge:

Rejoice in the Lord always. I will say it again: Rejoice! Let your gentleness be evident to all. The Lord is near. Do not be anxious about anything, but in everything, by prayer and petition, with thanksgiving, present your requests to God. And the peace of God, which transcends all understanding, will guard your hearts and minds in Christ Jesus. (Philippians 4:4-7)

There it is: the first step toward conflict resolution is to focus on your own relationship with God. But earlier in the letter, Paul provides even more insight into the matter:

Your attitude should be the same as that of Christ Jesus: Who, being in the very nature of God, did not consider equality with God something to be grasped, but made himself nothing, taking the very nature of a servant, being made in human likeness. And being found in appearance as a man, he humbled himself and became obedient to death—even death on a cross! (Philippians 2:5-8)

We do not know if these women ever resolved their conflict. What we are told, however, is that their conflict potentially divided a church that was otherwise filled with great joy. As we seek to resolve our own issues of marital conflict—or sibling conflict, or employer-employee conflict, or parent-child conflict—we must remember to grasp that eternal perspective and rejoice in the Lord, using Christ as our example, who displayed the very sort of humble attitude for which we ourselves should constantly strive. We must be always mindful of the gravity of the sin of unresolved conflict, and the destruction it brings to husbands and wives, brothers and sisters, parents and children. Eventually, it becomes a rotting corpse that nauseates the Church. The longer it's allowed to grow, the harder it is to remove.

Teaching Moments

- Tell your little ones this true story. When I was a little boy, we loved chasing baseballs from the little league games into the woods and returning them to the field of play. One day, I ran into the woods after a foul ball. This time, there were no other kids racing to the ball. There I stood, all alone in front of a brand new, shiny little league baseball with no one in sight. That is when I decided to hide the ball under the tree, return to the field later that night, and steal the ball. All I had to do was come up with a lie to tell my dad so he would drive me back to the field. So I told him that I forgot my glove and he kindly drove me back. I ran into the woods to fetch the stolen ball, only to see in the distance two pair of eyes, like little shiny stars, that looked like they belonged to two ferocious wolves. I froze, but they didn't. They sprinted after me and closed the gap, growling as they galloped, until I could hear them snort, feel the warmth of their saliva, and see their threatening fangs. They were poised at my belly. I was so scared, I couldn't even scream for my "daddy," who was waiting for me in the car. Just then, I heard a familiar voice. It was my little league manager who was walking his two German Shepherds in those woods. The wild wolf attack had just been my guilty imagination running away with me! He asked me the same question God asked Elijah the prophet when he sat alone in a cave, running away like a sick coward from Jezebel: "What are you doing here?" That was a question I will never forget. Ask your kids what they would have done in this situation.
- When our oldest son was a child, he suffered from nightmares. It was very painful to watch him, in the middle of the night, literally running from his imaginary devils. The by-product of these terrors was a stubbornly-entrenched doubt about his own salvation—a lie directly from Satan. He was able to be cured of this doubt by memorizing and meditating upon Romans 8:1-2: *Therefore,*

there is now no condemnation for those who are in Christ Jesus, because through Christ Jesus the law of the Spirit of life set me free from the law of sin and death. We used the only source of real truth—the Word of God—to let God Himself do the healing. What are your child's fears? How can you utilize the power of Scripture pertaining to that fear to bring about lasting freedom from those fears?

• The best and most effective way to teach children about the principle of resolving conflict is to resolve conflict the right way yourself. It is important for your children to see that you are a peaceful man or woman, that you know how to face opposition or deal with criticism, and that you know how to accept and work on your own blind spots when other people point them out to you. As a parent, you must strive to have a humble and gentle spirit, which is the complete opposite of the first of the deadly sins—*pride.*

• Refer to my sermon series on "The Missing Art of Church Discipline" to see how the Church ought to respond to egregious sin within the Body (visit www.markinc.org).

• Using the following verses from the Proverbs, reinforced as you deem appropriate, teach your kids the importance of accepting mediation or counseling to help resolve conflict:

He who heeds discipline shows the way to life, but whoever ignores correction leads others astray. (Proverbs 10:17)

The way of a fool seems right to him, but a wise man listens to advice. (Proverbs 12:15)

He who ignores discipline comes to poverty and shame, but whoever heeds correction is honored. (Proverbs 13:18)

Listen to advice and accept instruction, and in the end you will be wise. (Proverbs 19:20)

Apply your heart to instruction and your ears to words of knowledge. (Proverbs 23:12)

CHAPTER SIX
Raising Kids Who Stand Out in the Crowd

Teach Your Children This Story

DANIEL'S MIND WAS already made up.

Nebuchadnezzar, the king of Babylon, had invaded the land of Judah, and Daniel was one of the captives who'd been taken away to the king's palace. Along with several other bright and physically adept young men, he was ordered to undergo a three-year period of training before entering into royal service.

But to Daniel and his countrymen, Babylon was a place filled with strange people and even stranger idols. It represented a host of gods unfamiliar to Daniel who had no idea when—if ever—he would see his beloved homeland again. He determined in his heart, however, that he would *not* be defiled by the new pagan culture that surrounded him.

His first challenge came when he asked for permission to abstain from eating and drinking the royal food and wine, which, by the laws of his God, were forbidden to him. But when the guard refused, insisting that he would be blamed if they began looking worse than the other young men because of their failure to eat, Daniel replied with a challenge:

"Please test your servants for ten days: Give us nothing but vegetables to eat and water to drink. Then compare our appearance with that of the young men who eat the royal food, and treat your servants in accordance with what you see." (Daniel 1:12)

The guard agreed to the arrangement and, after ten days' time, Daniel and his friends did appear to be healthier and better-nourished than any of the other servants.

As the months and years passed in exile, Daniel grew in stature before the kings of Babylon—first King Nebuchadnezzar, then his son, Belshazzar, and finally King Darius. During Darius' reign, Daniel was elevated to one of the highest positions in the government, evoking great political jealousy. Some of the royal officials conspired secretly to discredit him and thus destroy his standing before the king. They searched and plotted, but could find nothing that they could possibly report to the king that would warrant Daniel's ouster. And although the thought probably occurred to them, these petty politicians understood that if they made false accusations against Daniel, it would bring serious punishment against them since the king loved and respected Daniel so much.

Their only remaining hope was to figure out a way that Daniel's own faith could be used against him—to find a way in which Daniel's faith came into direct conflict with the laws of the land. Then, Darius would be forced to punish him in order to keep face among the people. With this in mind, they approached King Darius with a scheme...

"The royal administrators, prefects, satraps, advisers and governors have all agreed that the king should issue an edict and enforce the decree that anyone who prays to any god or man during the next thirty days, except to you, O king, shall be thrown into the lions' den. Now, O king, issue the decree and put it in writing so that it cannot be

altered—in accordance with the laws of the Medes and Persians, which cannot be repealed." (Daniel 6:7-8)

The prideful king, not fully aware of all who would actually be affected by such a law, eagerly issued the decree. When Daniel heard about the decree, he threw himself before the God of Israel in prayer, thanked Him for the trial, and renewed his commitment not to bow before man-made idols or pray to false gods, regardless of the consequences he might have to face.

As was Daniel's custom, he would routinely face Jerusalem in his chamber and pray to his God, a faithful habit that his accusers soon discovered. Armed with the necessary "evidence," they slithered before the king and reminded him of the recent law he had passed forbidding prayer to anyone except him.

Then they said to the king, "Daniel, who is one of the exiles from Judah, pays no attention to you, O king, or to the decree you put in writing. He still prays three times a day." (Daniel 6:13)

The king was distressed at the news, since Daniel was one of his most valued and trusted advisors. He certainly didn't intend for him to die in the blood-curdling violence of the lion's den. Although the king desperately sought ways to save Daniel's life, the edict was irrevocable and allowed no exceptions. With nothing more that could be done, without great political cost, Darius very reluctantly gave the order to throw Daniel to the hungry beasts. The king legally sealed the large stone that was placed over the den's entrance with his signet ring, then dejectedly returned to the palace and spent the night in miserable sorrow.

Imagine this scene—the most powerful political leader in the then-known world awakes at dawn, rushes to the lions' den, and cries out in anguish, *"Daniel, servant of the living God, has your God, whom you serve continually, been able to rescue you from the lions?"* (Daniel 6:20)

Imagine his joy (and surprise) when the king heard a voice booming from behind the stone! *Daniel answered, "O king, live forever! My God sent his angel and he shut the mouths of the lions. They have not hurt me, because I was found innocent in his sight. Nor have I ever done any wrong before you, O king"* (Daniel 6:21-22). The king ordered that Daniel be removed from the den. Amazingly, after spending an entire night in a cave filled with hungry lions, not a single scratch or wound was found on him.

Darius commanded that Daniel's accusers be thrown into the lion's den where they received their due recompense—a violent death in the jaws of some very angry beasts. And Darius, legislating from his bench of absolute power, issued a new edict:

"I issue a decree that in every part of my kingdom people must fear and reverence the God of Daniel. For he is the living God and he endures forever; his kingdom will not be destroyed, his dominion will never end. He rescues and he saves; he performs signs and wonders in the heavens and on the earth. He has rescued Daniel from the power of the lions."

So Daniel prospered during the reign of Darius... (Daniel 6:25-28)

Parenting Principle: Your children must learn to stand alone.

In the book of Luke, we read about a special conversation that Jesus had with Peter during the last supper.

As they broke bread together, the Savior had a shocking, yet comforting, revelation for His disciple...

"Simon, Simon, Satan has asked to sift you as wheat. But I have prayed for you, Simon, that your faith may not fail. And when you have turned back, strengthen your brothers." (Luke 22:31)

Jesus lifted the veil of the invisible spirit-world for Peter to peek in and see that Satan, in Job-like fashion, had literally asked for God to take down His wall of protection around Peter so that the Evil One might attack him. However, Jesus was also praying for Peter that he would be able to withstand the enemy's assaults, emerge with his faith intact, and be armed to effectively minister to his brethren who were facing, or would soon face, similar temptations.

Every parent needs to take notice of a fearful and poignant truth: *Satan desires to sift your children, and is brazen enough to ask God to remove the hedges of protection around them.* Is it not terribly sobering that Satan knows how to pray for your children? Every day, there are forces of evil devoted to seeing that hedge of protection around your kids dismantled so that they might come at them with full fury. But it is also encouraging to know that these enemies must ask for permission, and that God has made this promise to you, a promise to which He will always remain faithful:

No temptation has seized you except what is common to man. And God is faithful; **he will not let you be tempted beyond what you can bear. But when you are tempted, he will also provide a way out** *so that you can stand up under it.* (1 Corinthians 10:13) (emphasis added)

At times we might feel as though the fires of testing are too hot, too much to bear, and too painful. And although God does not promise to take away the trial, He does promise to walk us through it. Before Daniel's lion encounter, his three friends, Shadrach, Meshach, and Abednego, in their commitment to stand alone when all others dropped to their knees to worship false gods, decided to stick out like the proverbial sore thumbs and refused to bow. The penalty for violating this law was that they were tossed into the fiery furnace that had been heated to seven times its normal temperature. This heat was so intense that the soldiers who escorted them to the doors of the furnace were instantly killed by the heat. Fully arrayed in their robes and turbans, the three young men were tossed into this deadly fire, with everyone expecting instant incineration. Surely, this would prove to be more than they could handle; surely, God had reneged on His promise. But then we read:

Then King Nebuchadnezzar leaped to his feet in amazement and asked his advisers, "Weren't there three men that we tied up and threw into the fire?" They replied, "Certainly, O king." He said, "Look! I see four men walking around in the fire, unbound, and unharmed, and the fourth looks like a son of the gods." (Daniel 3:24-25)

Put simply, their God—*our* God—jumped into the furnace with them, and although He did not remove the flames, He simply removed the effect of the heat.

Apparently, it was a lesson Peter never forgot. After Jesus' death and resurrection, the apostle would go on to warn young men to be self-controlled and alert, because *"your enemy the devil prowls around like a roaring lion looking for someone to devour"* (1 Peter 5:8). Satan is a ruthless enemy to our families.

Our kids are arguably living in one of the most morally-challenging cultures in all of history, where what is right and wrong has become clouded at best. Our 21st century moral furnace, heated seven times over, can and does overwhelm a child who has not been properly prepared to face such challenges—and many die at its doors. Modern communications such as the Internet, relational websites, cell phones, and a slew of emerging technologies have raised the thermostats in our modern moral furnaces even more. Moral borders that parents once guarded are now routinely crossed by kids who, just a generation ago, were babysat by the TV, watching *Sesame Street* in my children's generation and *Howdy Doody* in my own.

As Christian parents, we must teach our kids how to stand alone, how to endure the heat, and how to lean upon the One who will walk with them through the intensity of these morally challenging fires. Like Daniel and his friends, our children must learn how to stand out in the crowd while everyone else drops to their knees before their idols. But, the question is—how do they learn to do this? There are some critical principles you must teach them to grasp if they are to successfully stand alone in the midst of a strange and foreign culture.

In order to stand alone our children must learn dependence upon the Word of God.

My son, keep my words and store up my
commands within you. Keep my commands and
you will live; guard my teachings as the apple of your eye.
Bind them on your fingers; write them on the tablet
of your heart. Say to wisdom, "You are my sister,"
and call understanding your kinsman; they will
keep you from the adulteress, from the wayward
wife with her seductive words.
Proverbs 7:1-5

In this passage, the son had no business even being near the adulteress's neighborhood, but he was there anyway. As the nighttime approached, the young man strolled quietly in the direction of her house.

She came outside in full prostitute's regalia, moving flirtatiously towards him...

"I have fellowship offerings at home; today I fulfilled my vows," she said as she kissed him brazenly. "So I came out to meet you; I looked for you and have found you! I have covered my bed with colored linens from Egypt. I have perfumed my bed with myrrh, aloes and cinnamon. Come, let's drink deep of love until morning; let's enjoy ourselves with love! My husband is not at home; he has gone on a long journey. He took his purse filled with money and will not be home till full moon." (Proverbs 7:14-18)

It takes little imagination to see where this is heading—the young man is about to get into some serious moral trouble. But also notice that he had likely paid a visit to this woman's neighborhood before. He moved purposely in the direction of her house, and she had been looking for him. This was no mere "chance" meeting. His sin patterns had already formed, resulting in a lack of moral discernment. These entrenched habits are what dictated his decision to park himself on her corner as red meat for the hungry, roaring lion.

Let's take a moment to assess his situation. According to Jesus, there are two types of adultery that a person can commit: physical adultery and spiritual adultery (Matthew 5:27-30). Although this young man is about to commit the *physical* act of adultery, the broader picture in these verses portrays the evil snare of his *spiritual* adultery as well. And one of the roots of his downward moral spiral was his failure to believe in and apply the promises of God's Word found in Proverbs 7:1-5. Parents become culpable when they do not impress these Scriptures on the tablets of their child's heart and insist on personal accountability when evil lures them toward the corner of her house.

This is a principle that we must diligently teach our children. Dependence upon the Word of God means that the whole *mind* and the whole *heart* are to be occupied, or dare I say possessed, by the Word; in other words, the Scriptures should be the grid through which our children learn how to view life. If they are faithful to the words of Proverbs 7:1—that is, to *store up* the commands of the Scriptures—our children will know how to lay up God's Word in their hearts as a daily prescription for life, and not just store it on a shelf to be occasionally examined. When they faithfully store up the Word, they will not only inwardly hear its commands in moments of moral testing, but will also receive all of the blessed promises that come with obedience. In order to receive those promises, however, they must first understand what the promises *are*—especially the promise that speaks of deliverance from evil (Matthew 6:9-13, Luke 11:2-4), and what steps they should take to avoid falling into the trap of moral failure in the first place.

Strong dependence on the Word of God means that your children should also maintain a jealous regard for God's Law, or, as Proverbs 7:2 tells us, *"Keep my commands and you will live; guard my teachings as the apple of your eye."* To hold a debate with evil is the moment when we begin to fall into its deceptive snare, a la Eve's little conversation with the serpent. Contrariwise, our children will be able to stand against the tide of evil when they learn to guard the Word's commands without rationalizing its teachings or compromising its standards. The concept of right versus wrong is very clear in God's Word. When the Scriptures are carefully studied, and parents lovingly engrave its teachings on the tablets of their child's heart, the muddied waters of what is right and what is wrong will begin to clear up.

When it comes to these commands regarding the Word, we are also told to...

...bind them on your fingers; write them on the tablet of your heart. Say to wisdom, "You are my sister," and call understanding your kinsman; they will keep you from the adulteress, from the wayward wife with her seductive words. (Proverbs 7:3-5)

In other words, these verses tell us that we must be prepared to *deploy* what we learn in the Scriptures. We are to love God's teachings, understand them thoroughly, and take comfort in them as we would a trusted friend. What good does it do us to have a rifle in hand when the enemy engages us on the battlefield if we don't know how to use it? In the same manner, we should know how to effectively use God's Word as a weapon in the face of moral temptation. Satan is not intimidated by our mere Scriptural knowledge or that we can quote chapter and verse. When the Word is engrafted on our children's hearts, they will be prepared to do battle with whatever the world throws at them.

In order to stand alone, our children must learn how to translate the truth of Scripture into the practicum of everyday life.

To spot a counterfeit dollar bill, one must be totally familiar with the real deal. Once the image of the true has been engrained, a counterfeit will stick out like a sore thumb. Similarly, our children must learn to spot the counterfeit by ingraining the truth of God's Word in them. Throughout the Proverbs, we are continuously reminded of the need to possess *Wisdom, understanding,* and *judgment.* Although these terms are closely related, they are not exactly the same. They are fluid in nature.

In chapter 1, we learned that a good working definition of *Wisdom* is to view life through the grid of Scripture. *Wisdom* is the *logos* or Word of God—the Word by which God has been revealed to us is Christ (John 1:1, 14). In other words, Jesus is the physical revelation of God, the incarnation of God. If we desire *Wisdom*, we must know Christ. The Scriptures are the written revelation of God. If you want to know what God thinks (*Wisdom*) we must desire to know the Scriptures. *Wisdom* is truth. When your child is dealing with the temptation to steal, for example, there should be no debate about the right or wrong of it. Stealing is wrong because God's Word says it is. Stealing is morally unacceptable, and that's the Wisdom of God.

But, mere Bible knowledge is not enough. The *Wisdom* or *logos* of God must be practical. The *ethos* or *understanding* represents the ethical demands of Scripture, or the application of what God says is true. When your child has understanding, he will be able to put "feet" to his theology and will know how to act on the already acquired truth. *Understanding* is how the Word applies to everyday life.

Judgment is the key to effectively helping your child assess his or her options when facing a specific situation. It teaches them to ask some key questions. What are my moral choices? What are the consequences of each of those choices? How did I get into this situation in the first place? Is this where God wants me? Do I have any business being here? Have I violated the Scriptures? What steps must I now take?

All three of these qualities—*Wisdom, understanding,* and *judgment*—taught to your children in tandem is what will shape their *worldview*, the grid through which they see life. If their minds are filled with Scriptural content but they are never taught how to ethically apply that content or assess their environment, then they will not be equipped to effectively deal with the Evil One. However, when your children possess these qualities, they will grow to become young adults who truly fear God, hate the things that He hates, and will be able to stand alone in the most critical moments of their lives.

In order to stand alone our children must learn the danger of mental loitering.

Throughout my years of preaching, there have been many times when, in the middle of a sermon, I have looked out and noticed *them*—men and women I knew were not paying the least bit of attention to what I was saying. They have that blank stare that advertises that they're thinking about something else, or that they're not thinking at all. They drift away from everything they *should* be thinking about. Their minds have vacated the truth, they have become spiritual loiterers.

Any good teacher will tell you that, when they look out into the sea of young faces over the rows of desks, they can easily spot the one who is paying absolutely no attention. That student clearly *needs* that instruction, but because her mind has drifted and is not focused on the words of her teacher or the notes on the board, she will not be prepared for the upcoming final exam.

The same applies to the spiritual lives of our children. When they stroll idly through life with vacant and loitering minds, they will *never* be able to stand alone. A vacant and loitering mind means that a child's guard has been let down. The spiritual restraint that would normally keep him from wandering into a bad situation is loosened. Without moral restraints, our children can very easily begin a spiral into moral failure. Solomon reinforces the need for his son to pay attention:

My son, pay attention to what I say; listen closely to my words. Do not let them out of your sight, keep them within your heart; for they are life to those who find them and health to a man's whole body. (Proverbs 4:20-22)

From early childhood through adolescence, our children crave behavioral borders. The unhappiest children are the ones with no borders. Without parentally-imposed and Scripturally-based borders, our children will mentally loiter. Excessive freedom and permissiveness is the playground where the evil stranger (Satan) lures our kids into his car where he intends to do them great harm. Godly borders are cultivated in the fertile soil of your child's soul. That is the field where wise parents sow the seeds of Scripturally-imposed external restraints on their child's behavior and friendships, fertilize that seed with the Scriptural and parental consequences for disobedience and/or the blessings of obedience, and then prune the growing plants with a pathway forward if and when there is failure. Then, as our children internalize God's warnings and promises, we watch them grow into adulthood and hopefully pick the fruit in our legacy. This is my working definition of early childhood discipline.

As a father, I never promised my children that I would never tell them, "I told you so." In fact, I promised my children that I would *always* tell them "I told you so!" Ironically, our adult children would tell you that that very fact seemed to become an incentive to obedience in and of itself. I always made sure to remind my growing children that, someday, they were going to need the words of instruction that I gave them.

But Solomon has more to say about the matter in Proverbs 4...

Let your eyes look straight ahead, fix your gaze directly before you. Make level paths for your feet and take only ways that are firm. Do not swerve to the right or the left; keep your foot from evil. (Proverbs 4:25-27)

As this passage emphasizes, just as race horses wear blinders to help them focus on the finish line, our children must always wear blinders, figuratively speaking, to keep them focused on their goals and God-ordained purpose in life. When they mentally loiter, the blinders fall off, and their worldview becomes skewed and warped. When this happens, the finish line is no longer in sight and our children begin to walk a morally dangerous line. And in the blink of an eye, they end up in a place where they do not belong.

In order to stand alone our children must learn not to run spiritual yellow lights.

In the state of Delaware, we now have cameras at almost every traffic light. This means that, if a light turns from yellow to red while you are driving through that intersection, you can expect to receive a letter in the mail a few days later, along with instructions on how to pay the sizeable fine you now owe for not taking a yellow light seriously. You slipped through while you thought no one was watching. Likewise, our children must learn the importance of recognizing those spiritual yellow lights in their own lives or they will not be able to stand alone. And the fine is much stiffer than they realize.

The young man from Proverbs 7 is seen wandering down to *her*, the adulteress woman's corner in the fading light of evening. When she finally came out to greet him, she told him she had *"fellowship offerings at home,"* because she had *"fulfilled her vows that day"* (Proverbs 7:14). In one fell swoop, this deceptive woman managed to "spin" her sin by somehow claiming that what they were about to do was right, since she had paid her vows. The "good" works that she did that day would surely outweigh the bad things they were about to do. Right? Wrong!

The young man in this scenario seems to fall for this deception, hook, line and sinker. All too quickly, he forgot his father's warnings about the consequences of wandering mental focus. Despite the urgent advice that implored him not to even begin to turn in her direction, this boy chose to ignore the flashing yellow light right in front of him and run the red light.

Our children are faced with scores of yellow lights every day warning them of the dangers of lying, stealing, drug use and a host of other things. We must teach them to stand alone, especially when under intense peer pressure. We must not fail to teach them the importance of recognizing when a spiritual yellow light is flashing so that they may properly assess the moral environment and imminent challenges they face. Contrary to what one might think, sin does not initially occur when we actually run the red light and commit the evil deed. It starts well before that when we see the flashing yellow light and make the decision to hit the accelerator. That is, sin occurs at the precise moment we make the first mental movement or serious contemplation toward the immoral activity. This young man's sin first occurred when he made the conscious decision to turn down the street toward her neighborhood.

In order to stand alone our children must learn the deception of the pleasant appearance of sin.

In Proverbs 7, we find our young man enticed by some very pleasant-sounding words from the adulterous woman:

"I have covered my bed with colored linens from Egypt. I have perfumed my bed with myrrh, aloes and cinnamon. Come, let's drink deep of love until morning; let's enjoy ourselves with love!" (Proverbs 7:16)

This allure of sin is deceptive, and it sounded good to this boy, but he failed to remember that...

For the lips of an adulteress drip honey, and her speech is smoother than oil; but in the end she is bitter as gall, sharp as a double-edged sword. Her feet go down to death; her steps lead straight to the grave. She gives no thought to the way of life; her paths are crooked, but she knows it not. (Proverbs 5:3-6)

Sin, at least initially, can taste as sweet as honey. This deceptive "honey" can show up in your child's idols and heroes. They can easily be mesmerized by the allure of stardom. How do your kids dress? Who are their friends? Are they preoccupied with the perceived "glamour" of underage drinking, sex, and the like? Did you catch that in Proverbs 5:5? *Her feet go down to death.* Death–spiritual, emotional, and even physical death! The aroma, the taste, the touch, and the fake aura of sin's pleasure will open wide the mouth of the grave in the hopes of swallowing our kids.

In order to stand alone our children must reject the notion of any such thing as a secret sin.

"No one will ever know..."
"I'm sure I won't get caught..."
"I'll keep this a secret..."
These are the lines of reasoning we often rehearse in our minds when we are thinking about committing, or have already committed, some sin that we believe or hope no one will ever discover. It's certainly the belief system that caused the young man in Proverbs 7 to fall for the adulterous woman. Look again at what she tells him...

"My husband is not at home; he has gone on a long journey. He took his purse filled with money and will not be home till full moon." (Proverbs 7:19-20)

What is she saying here? *When we go behind closed doors, no one else is going to know about this...it'll be our little secret.* As he follows her into her house, he has, once again, apparently forgotten the fundamental principle his father taught him...

The fear of the Lord is the beginning of knowledge, but fools despise wisdom and discipline. (Proverbs 1:7)

Like this boy, our children will not stand alone if they believe that there is such a thing as a "secret" sin, or that there is some offense, large or small, that they can commit without anyone noticing it. But even when no one else is around to witness their actions, our children must remember that God does, in fact, see and know everything—and if they truly fear Him, the knowledge of this fact will influence everything they do—for life!

Nowhere is your child's ability to stand alone more consequential than in the company of his peers, outside your supervision. Most of us know of parents who have lost the attention and affections of their children to the power of peer pressure, in spite of their best efforts to raise their kids up in the way they should go. Our human nature— your child's nature—craves popularity and acceptance, and he will be tempted to make moral compromises to achieve it. The principles outlined here are among your most effective tools for arming your child to stand out and stand alone.

In order to stand alone our children must learn there are consequences to moral failure.

Have you ever driven past a truckload of cows or chickens on the highway? More than likely, you know where those animals are going—to a cold slaughterhouse for butchering.

That's exactly how our naïve and undiscerning young man in Proverbs 7 is described...

With persuasive words she led him astray; she seduced him with her small talk. All at once he followed her like an ox going to the slaughter, like a deer stepping into a noose till an arrow pierces his liver, like a bird darting into a snare, little knowing it will cost him his life. (Proverbs 7:21-23)

There is a pretty strong metaphor contained in these verses, and rightly so. The moment this boy grew comfortable with the coiled snake in front of him, it jumped out and bit him before he even realized what was happening. Our children should understand that the consequences of sin are often severe, and they can come at a moment's notice. Before we know it, we can find ourselves trapped like chickens on a farmer's truck, with heads happily bobbing, feathers flying...and imminent slaughter awaiting them.

In Proverbs 5, Solomon warned his son beforehand of these consequences...

...lest you give your best strength to others and your years to one who is cruel, lest strangers feast on your wealth and your toil enrich another man's house. At the end of your life you will groan, when your flesh and body are spent. You will say, "How I hated discipline! How my heart spurned correction! I would not obey my teachers or listen to my instructors. I have come to the brink of utter ruin in the midst of the whole assembly." (Proverbs 5:9-14)

But again, parents, be warned by a subtle implication contained in this passage: it is at the *end of your life you will groan when your flesh and body are spent*. It is altogether possible that the consequences of sin may not be immediate. The danger is that immoral behavior and sins done in secret can become reinforced, habitual behavior when we or our children rationalize "I got away with it!" But a heart that has God's law engraved on it from childhood is far less prone to start down this fatal path of self-deception.

Proverbs 7 is a portrait of a young man who just didn't "get it." Not unlike our young kids, he either didn't understand or did not remember the crucial principles that would have helped him stand alone in the face of great moral temptation, and that is what snared him into choosing a joyride to the slaughter house. Standing against the surge of immorality will rarely be easy for our children. Yet, the moral victory of standing alone is *always* possible when they learn and apply these seven critical core principles.

Are you raising a Daniel who will dare to stand when all others kneel before the gods of moral failure?

Teaching Moments

• To help your child understand the consequences of moral failure and the importance of making the right choices in the face of temptation, sit down and teach them the testimonies of those who fell as a result of their sin. Bible references such as the story of Gehazi (2 Kings 5) and the story of Ananias and Sapphira (Acts 5) are especially effective for communicating this principle.

• Be willing to explore, with age appropriateness, the publicized moral failings of modern-day celebrities and other well-known people with whom your kids may be infatuated.

• Teach your child how to instantly obey. To help our children learn submission to our authority and thus how to submit to God's law, as well as God-ordained authorities later in life, we often practiced teaching them how to respond to our instructions in every possible situation. Sometimes we said "no" in order to test their instant obedience. I often told them the story of the dad and son who were hiking. The dad suddenly yelled, "Don't move!" His son's submission to his dad's authority was so complete that he instantly stood perfectly still. If he had seen what his father saw, his natural instincts to run from danger might have caused great harm or even death, for hidden in the grass at his feet was a dangerous, poisonous snake. Another example is the story of a child about to run across a street. His mother yells, "Stop!" He almost falls in his attempt to instantly obey, *even though he doesn't know why his mother yelled.* If he had not listened, he would have run into the pathway of a speeding car. Use every day examples to teach your children to instantly obey.

• Monitor with laser-like precision your child's time and activity on the Internet. Use content-discerning software with guards and passwords in place. These websites, whether we like it or not, represent the people who are becoming your child's friends on places like MySpace and Facebook. Their "Space" needs to become your "Space" and their "Face" needs to become your "Face." Also, be very careful with their cell phones. Limit their use. Limit their privacy. Texting is a very popular method of communication among kids today. Read their text messages. *You* are the responsible parent—there should be little concern for their "privacy rights." The Bible describes it this way:

He who spares the rod hates his son, but he who loves him is careful to discipline him. (Proverbs 13:24)

Folly is bound up in the heart of a child, but the rod of discipline will drive it far from him. (Proverbs 22:15)

•   There is no greater need today than the parental oversight and discipline of the technological revolution. Parents must learn what are the newest trends and the secret "language" of the Internet. I guarantee you that your kids either know that language or soon will.

CHAPTER SEVEN
Your Child's Spiritual Birth Line

NOTE: The concept of The Spiritual Birth Line, or Ordo Saludis (order of salvation), as it is called, has been a subject of debate by Christian scholars for centuries. The reader may find some of the material in this chapter unfamiliar or challenging to understand, but the fundamental doctrines of our historic Christian faith, centered on salvation through repentance and faith in Christ alone, are in no way brought into question. The topic is introduced here as a useful tool for instructing parents that raising children is a spiritual marathon and not a spiritual sprint—a rewarding effort over the long haul, not "shortcuts" that may be based on misunderstandings of the nature of God's plan of salvation. It is my fervent prayer that this chapter will stimulate your thinking to further investigate these truths for yourself.

Teach Your Children This Story

ONE DAY, WHILE Jesus was having dinner at a Jewish leader's home, He decided to tell a story...

Now, Jesus was a rather good storyteller—as a matter of fact, He often used stories (also called parables) to teach His followers some very important lessons about life. On this particular day, the story He told was about a very wealthy man who decided to throw a lavish banquet in his home. (Luke 14:15-23)

After much preparation, the man finally told his servant to announce to all his invited guests that the banquet was ready—this would surely be an occasion unlike any they had ever experienced. But surprisingly, the guests all gave a variety of last-minute excuses as to why they couldn't attend the feast. *"I have just bought a field, and I must go and see it," said one. "I have just bought five yoke of oxen, and I'm on my way to try them out. Please excuse me," said another.* One invitee offered an even stranger explanation for not coming. *"I just got married, so I can't come"* (Luke 14:18-20).

When the servant returned and reported that the guests would not be attending the banquet, the master was furious. *"Go out quickly into the streets and alleys of the town and bring in the poor, the crippled, the blind and the lame," he ordered* (Luke 14:21). The servant did as he was told, and hurried out in search of new guests for the feast. One by one, the town's poorest and most bedraggled men and women came and took their places beside the mountains of food, humbly grateful for this rare chance to enjoy it themselves.

After these new guests arrived, the servant said to his master, *"Sir, what you ordered has been done, but there is still room"* (Luke 14:22). The master instructed his servant to *"Go out to the roads and country lanes and make them come in, so that my house will be full. I tell you, not one of those men who were invited will get a taste of my banquet"* (Luke 14:23).

What a sight that must have been! Imagine dozens of poor and handicapped people sitting down in front of the most elegant meals they ever had, in the midst of a glorious banquet hall beyond anything they could wish for in their wildest dreams. Who would have thought they would ever partake in such an event? And it was all because, when they were invited, they responded quickly and respectfully to the call to come and sit down at the master's table.

Parenting Principle: Raising Godly children is a spiritual marathon and not a spiritual sprint.

Does not wisdom call out? Does not understanding raise her voice? On the heights along the way, where the paths meet, she takes her stand; beside the gates leading into the city, at the entrances, she cries aloud: "To you, O men, I call out; I raise my voice to all mankind."
Proverbs 8:1-4

Proverbs 8 is the "Grand Canyon" of the first nine chapters of Proverbs that are the focus of this book. My wife, Sharon, and I took a trip to the Grand Canyon a few years ago. I remember it well since, that day, I experienced the most excruciating migraine headache I'd ever had (and I have had many). But once I peered over the edge and saw this divine mosaic, it became surreal. It was amazing and breathtaking. I actually forgot for a moment how much pain I was in when I looked down and saw this masterpiece from the creative hand of my Lord and Savior. It truly was one of the big pictures of God's unfathomable genius.

Proverbs 8 gives us the big picture for the task of raising children. That is, on close examination of this chapter, one will see the macro-picture of successful childrearing. It can be a surreal experience! It is in Proverbs chapter 8 where we encounter the "meaty" characteristics of the Gospel. It is the heart and soul of the first nine chapters. It is here where we find, in all its glorious, panoramic view, the vital attributes of the Gospel message that we must commit ourselves to teaching our children before they reach adulthood.

Many no longer understand exactly what the Gospel means, or even what the Gospel *is*. However, we must faithfully teach our young children the Gospel principles found in Proverbs 8 so that they grow up and never remember a day when they *weren't* believers in Christ. I know this may startle some who believe that a dramatic point X, a conversion moment where a man or a woman comes to faith in Jesus Christ, is essential to salvation. And certainly, there must be a point X when we receive God's provision for our sins—His Son—and full assurance that we are saved. But a dramatic experience or a memorable encounter does not necessarily correspond to a true conversion. This is the promise of the covenant God made with Abraham, and Abraham's children after him, in Genesis 17:1-7:

When Abram was ninety-nine years old, the Lord appeared to him and said, "I am God Almighty; walk before me and be blameless. I will confirm my covenant between me and you and will greatly increase your numbers." Abram fell facedown, and God said to him, "As for me, this is my covenant with you: You will be the father of many nations. No longer will you be called Abram; your name will be Abraham, for I have made you a father of many nations. I will make you very fruitful; I will make nations of you, and kings will come from you. I will establish my covenant as an everlasting covenant between me and you and your descendants after you for the generations to come, to be your God and the God of your descendants after you."

Space prohibits me from laying out here the entire theological rationale behind the concept of one's Spiritual Birth Line. But it is presented in enough detail, with Scriptural references, that I'm hoping the reader will find it to be extremely enlightening in his desire to understand the deeper truths of God's salvation plan—with solid Biblical insights that you may not have considered before. So, I trust that what you are about to read will stretch your spiritual brain cells and prove to be a "theological safari" that you and your children will find rewarding! For those who would like to dig deeper, some follow up study would be time well spent (see **Teaching Moments** at the end of this chapter for some further discussion.).

Before beginning our walk through the inner workings of your Spiritual Birth Line, I want to offer some further introductory comments and summarize a few key foundational principles upon which the Birth Line concept is built. (A helpful illustration of "Your Spiritual Birth Line" is shown in Figure 1):

• This will be new material for many of my readers who are accustomed to equating being "born again" with being "saved" or "converted." As you will see later, this *may* be the case for some but *may not* be for others. Although one can be "born again" and "converted" at the same time, *it does not usually happen that way.* These are related though not identical terms. (Stay with me here!)

• The term "born again," in its New Testament context, refers only to a point in time when the Holy Spirit brings to life, or, as the English Puritans used to say, "quickens," a soul that was once spiritually dead and thus incapable of responding to the Gospel. This is a supernatural act of the Holy Spirit whereby He gives to us the faculty of faith and the gift of repentance to enable us to see our depravity before a Holy God and our need for a Savior. Some scholars prefer to use the term "regeneration" to describe this divine invasion. Regardless of the term used, the once-dead soul is miraculously brought to life and given the *ability* to exercise repentance and faith in Christ. Before this act of God, the dead soul possessed no ability at all to respond to the Gospel.

• This "quickening" or "born again" experience has been often misunderstood to mean "saved" or "converted," when in fact these are independent events that may occur simultaneously at God's discretion. It really means the one who once had no interest in the things of God, now has an interest. The one who had no desire or ability to exercise faith now does; the one who could not choose Christ now has the ability to do so. The one who could not and would not repent now becomes sensitive to the Holy Spirit's conviction of sin and will eventually feel the need to truly repent.

• "Conversion" or "salvation" occurs when the Holy Spirit draws, or *calls*, the newly regenerated soul to the cross where, in faith, and by God's sheer Mercy and Grace, he or she repents of their sins and receives Christ as Savior and Lord of their lives.

• Some confusion arises over the fact that God can, at His sole discretion, allow a period of time between the quickening (born again) and the conversion (salvation), *or* He can accomplish them simultaneously. Since we cannot see what's taking place in a person's soul, the distinction between these two "options" is invisible to us and known only by God.

• The bottom line is that, even with all of the above complexities taking place in God's invisible world, the simple truth of the Gospel still holds: *"Unless you are born again, you will not see the Kingdom of God"* (John 3:3). More on this verse later. Well-intentioned believers may differ over the details of the Birth Line concept, but it may be nothing more than a matter of semantics and questions of timing. "Traditionalists" need have no fear!

• Although God can and does save some in one dramatic moment, salvation is normally a process that occurs along a Spiritual Birth Line.

• Although I propose that there is normally an *ordo saludis* (order, or process, of salvation), God is never bound by any one spiritual process or timeline in salvation. For example, David's infant son had no ability to proceed through any birth line, yet after the infant's death, David knew the boy was in heaven and that he would see his son again (2 Samuel 12:15-23).

• One cannot have full assurance of salvation until he or she has repented of their sins and in faith has trusted in

Christ and Christ alone for their salvation. This is what it means to be truly converted.

• As I have taught the Birth Line over the years, there have been some common questions and objections raised. For example, what happens to babies who die in infancy? Or what happens to the mentally challenged? Or, what happens if someone dies before the Birth Line process is completed? Space does not permit me to do justice to all of the aspects of the Spiritual Birth Line concept, or answer all of the related questions here. A full examination of the topic, along with questions, is addressed in my extensive sermon series. (See **Teaching Moments** below). However, I believe we must entrust such people into the hands of a merciful and loving God who does all things well. He promised to save all of His people, and not one of them will be lost. Parents may take great comfort in that hope, especially those who suffer with rebellious children. Since we are all on a spiritual journey, as long as we are alive that journey has not ended and the hope of the Gospel remains.

• Understanding the norm of the salvation process will better equip you to guide your child through this journey, as well as give you hope along the way.

So let's begin to take a look at the Spiritual Birth Line (Figure 1).

Our children are on a spiritual journey, a Spiritual Birth Line that has its roots in the **eternal covenant of redemption** between the three Persons of the Trinity, before the foundation of the world. Nowhere in Scripture is the doctrine of the Trinity articulated better than in Ephesians chapter 1. Each of the three Persons of the Trinity has a specific role in redemption. There, we learn that the Father covenanted to save a people and elected them to eternal life (Ephesians 1:3-6); the Son covenanted to pay the penalty for the sins of these people, since we cannot save ourselves, by shedding His blood on the cross (Ephesians 1:7-12); and the Holy Spirit covenanted to individually apply the work of Christ by calling and converting the ones

God determined, in Grace, to save (Ephesians 1:12-14). So that we can better understand it, the several tasks of the work of the Spirit can be loosely mapped out using a sequential time line, or "Spiritual Birth Line" as in Figure 1. With the help of the material presented in this chapter, parents would do well to study their own birth line so as to better equip their children to understand theirs.

What God purposed in eternity past, must be made effectual in time in the heart of your child. The process begins when the Holy Spirit **regenerates** our depraved and wicked hearts. It comes at that moment when God's Holy Spirit intervenes in our dead and wicked hearts and gives us the ability to believe and to repent, the two indispensable acts by which one must be saved. All men are born with a sin nature (Psalm 51:5, Romans 3:23), making it impossible for them to respond to the call of the Gospel unless the Holy Spirit brings the dead spiritual corpse back to life (Ephesians 2:4-5). This is the miracle of regeneration, or what happens when one is "born again." The Holy Spirit is not random in regenerating dead souls back to life. He does so according to the plan—the eternal covenant of redemption.

Nicodemus, a great spiritual leader of the Sanhedrin, came to Jesus and was troubled by Jesus' message of repentance and faith. Jesus told him that *"No one can see the kingdom of God unless he is born again"* (John 3:3). The idea of a second birth troubled the practical-minded Nicodemus, causing him to wonder how a man can *"enter a second time into his mother's womb to be born"* (John 3:4). Just as Nicodemus missed the entire essence of this concept, so has the Church. In the original Greek language we discover that the words, *he must be born again*, involve not something that we do, but something that God does to us—this is the work of the Holy Spirit. The words literally translate: *"I tell you the truth, if one is not generated from above, he is not able to see the kingdom of God"* (John 3:3).

140

One may or may not necessarily be aware of when he or she has been born again, since it is a spiritual act, totally initiated by the Holy Spirit. It can happen at any point in one's life. It can be dramatic or not. Many of those early childhood moments, when a little one "prays to receive Jesus," may or may not actually be their true conversion–an event that usually comes later in the development of their Spiritual Birth Line. I remember many times, as a little child, when I was moved by Christ's incredible love to endure the cross for me. Now that I look back, I am convinced that I was **regenerated** or **"born again"** during one of those very special moments. It came during Easter, when I was about seven years old. I was *not* converted at that moment, but I was given *the ability to be converted* when the Holy Spirit took my dead soul, brought it back to life, and gave me faith to believe. My "conversion," when I exercised my Spirit-given capacity to repent and believe the Gospel, would actually occur twelve years later, when I was nineteen and in college.

Moving along the Birth Line, once a person is **regenerated**, or "born from above," the Holy Spirit calls them to the cross. There are many divine invasions that may occur along the way. I call these "divine scorch marks" that leave an indelible mark on the soul. Personally, I have identified twelve such scorch marks in my spiritual pilgrimage. These are the positive and negative events and circumstances God uses to lead us to the cross where we can be truly converted.

Our children hear the **call** in a variety of ways. It may come in the form of a sermon, a Sunday school lesson, another person's testimony, or any of a thousand other ways. But there is no way more meaningful for a child than to hear the call of the Gospel through the lips of moms and dads who daily point them to the cross. It is important to note that parents must be careful not to force a false conversion, where the child is either overtly resistant or does not properly understand the meaning of the Gospel. To do so is to risk a premature birth or even a still birth. Patiently teach your kids the truth and trust that the Holy Spirit will make it clear in His time, when He has made them "ready."

The next stop along the journey of one's Spiritual Birth Line is the moment of **conversion**. Conversion by definition is the marriage between repentance and faith in Christ. One must turn away from sin (repentance) and turn toward Christ (faith). It is a two-sided coin. One cannot be saved by "turning over a new leaf." This is false repentance, merely a man-made feeling of "sorrow or regret" and an effort to change one's behavior in an attempt to please God. Nor can one be saved by promising God that you'll do better or work harder. This is false faith.

To be genuinely **converted** we must acknowledge our sinful condition, that our sins are offensive to our Holy God, and that we deserve His displeasure. Then, in sincere **repentance**, we must turn away from our sins and in **faith** trust in Christ as the only One who can satisfy the justice of God. Then, and only then, are we ready to receive Jesus as our Savior and Lord by inviting Him into our lives.

It is at this point, that God desires that we have full assurance of eternal life...

And this is the testimony: God has given us eternal life, and this life is in his Son. He who has the Son has life; he who does not have the Son of God does not have life. I write these things to you who believe in the name of the Son of God so that you may know that you have eternal life. (1 John 5:11-13)

At the moment of **conversion** God **adopts** us as His children, marking us as His sons and daughters (Romans 8:15-17), **seals** us with His Holy Spirit as a deposit, guaranteeing eternal life to come (Ephesians 1:13-14), and **justifies** us, declaring us righteous under the Law (Romans 3:23-26)–"just as if" I'd never sinned. From the point of **conversion** onward, God daily empowers us by His Holy

Spirit to change and become more conformed to the image of Christ as He readies us for eternal life. This process, driven by the study of the Scriptures, is called **sanctification** (John 17:17). And when our life is scheduled to end, God promises that the work of salvation will be completed and we will be perfected as He brings us into His presence in Glory. Then and only then—in His presence—will we be **glorified**. This is when it will all make sense—all of the pain, all of the heartache, all of the suffering, and all of the brokenness.

However, as it is written: "No eye has seen, no ear has heard, no mind has conceived what God has prepared for those who love him." (1 Corinthians 2:9)

Perhaps there isn't a more concise summary of the Spiritual Birth Line than...

And we know that in all things God works for the good of those who love him, who have been called according to his purpose. For those God foreknew he also predestined to be conformed to the likeness of his Son, that he might be the firstborn among many brothers. And those he <u>predestined</u>, he also <u>called</u>; those he <u>called</u>, he also <u>justified</u>; those he <u>justified</u>, he also <u>glorified</u>. (Romans 8:28-30) (emphasis added)

All of these emphasized verbs are in the past tense. This is true even of our "future" **glorification**. In the heart and mind of God, it is guaranteed as if it already happened. How can this be? Actually, how can it *not* be, given the fact that God ordained our salvation in that great eternal covenant of redemption before the world was even made. Remember, in God's eternal view of time, each of our lives, and the events of our lives—past, present and future—are all visible to Him at once, as one intricate, hand-made tapestry. He transcends time (Psalm 90:4).

We can schematically represent the Spiritual Birth Line as shown in Figure 1.

(handwritten margin note: "Do you want to put your trust in God?")

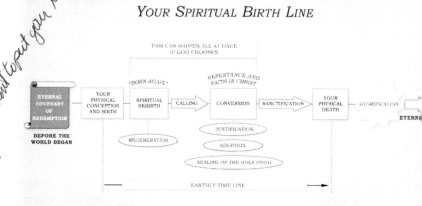

Figure 1. *Your Spiritual Birth Line*

Before we teach the concept of the **Spiritual Birth Line** to our children, there are two key theological concepts that we first must understand about this life-changing message.

The Gospel is to be proclaimed to all men everywhere.

> *Does not wisdom call out? Does not understanding*
> *raise her voice? On the heights along the way,*
> *where the paths meet, she takes her stand;*
> *beside the gates leading into the city, at the entrances,*
> *she cries aloud: "To you, O men, I call out;*
> *I raise my voice to all mankind."*
> Proverbs 8:1-4

As we have discussed previously, *Wisdom* personified is Jesus Christ. So when we read these first four verses of

Proverbs 8, we can interpret them to mean that *Jesus* (i.e., *Wisdom*) is calling out to us through the Holy Spirit.

Now, there are a few notable things to mention here. First, throughout Proverbs, Solomon implores us to hear *Wisdom calling out in the streets*. Would Wisdom (i.e., Jesus) cry out so loud, or continue crying for so long, if there were not a terrible wrath that awaits your child's soul should she fail to embrace the cross and come to truly know Him? The fact is that Jesus suffered the equivalent of an eternity in hell for the sins of His people. Thus, He cries out in the streets for all men to hear that there is a heaven to be gained and a hell to be shunned. God help this hell-bound world when that merciful call falls silent and the invitation is closed.

Second, notice that the Gospel call is extended to *all mankind*. Your kids must learn that, like the poor and handicapped in the parable of the great banquet feast (Luke 14:15-24), they have been *invited* to a great feast. With every sermon or testimony they hear, every Sunday school or youth group lesson they learn, every devotional you lead them in at home, *they are being invited to heed the call of the Gospel*. And if they fail to respond, there is no doubt that they will one day stand before God and account for every sermon they refused to listen to, for each and every time they ignored family devotions, or for every mocking response to the urgings of their teachers.

Third, one might inquire how God, at the same time, orchestrates the Spiritual Birth Line *and* holds the sinner responsible for their sin. If God is in control of salvation, then why will He hold me accountable? It is unmistakable that the Bible teaches both doctrines—God is sovereign and man is responsible. How do we square these two truths? We don't! These great truths form two parallel lines that cross somewhere above us in the mysteries of the Godhead. But, take comfort, reader!—one of the greatest theological minds of Scripture, the Apostle Paul himself, recognized this "paradox" between God's sovereignty and man's personal responsibility, and left us with no recourse but to bow humbly at the feet of our Sovereign Potter...

"One of you will say to me: 'Then why does God still blame us? For who resists his will?' But who are you, O man, to talk back to God? Shall what is formed say to him who formed it, 'Why did you make me like this?' Does not the potter have the right to make out of the same lump of clay some pottery for noble purposes and some for common use?" (Romans 9: 19-21)

The initial invitees in this great parable refused to attend the banquet, so the master ordered the servants to invite others in their place. The invitation went out in the mail, not in the form of letters with postage stamps, but as living letters sent into the cities and the suburbs. *"Go out to the roads and country lanes and make them come in"* (Luke 14:24). As Christians, it is our job, our *responsibility*, our *obligation*, to take God's message of hope into the world, into the streets and highways of the cities and into the roads and lanes of the countryside, to proclaim the good news that Christ has redeemed us from the slimy, stench-filled pit of sin and death.

And this message must be owned by your children. It is to that little boy or girl—God's heritage on loan to you— that you must, with all of your heart, consistently and faithfully proclaim the Gospel and lead them to the cross. But understand that, from birth, we do not naturally or willingly seek God. We avoid Him. And no one can be led to the cross who will not first acknowledge his hopelessly lost, sinful condition before a just and Holy God. Excuse-making is inbred in the heart of every child. "He did it," "Let's make a deal," or "Let me explain" may lead to the more serious excuse-making as an adult: "No thanks, I am glad Jesus works for you. I'm not as bad as some other people I know!"

Children despise having to admit guilt. But many children never grow up and continue to avoid guilt and admission of wrongdoing all their lives. As adults, they often destroy relationships with spouses, co-workers, bosses, or even fellow church members, simply because they refuse to take responsibility for wrongs they've done to others. They become experts at creating logical explanations for their mistakes. Is there then any doubt as to why they will also refuse to admit their sinful guilt before God? John tells us...

If we confess our sins, he is faithful and just and will forgive us our sins and purify us from all unrighteousness. (1 John 1:9)

Confession—what did John mean by that word? To *confess* means *to agree with God.* Apart from agreeing and admitting (confessing) sin, there will be no true repentance. One cannot repent for something when, in his heart, he does not believe he is guilty. Without repentance there can be no faith, and *without faith it is impossible to please God* (Hebrews 11:6). Confession begins when our children admit to raiding the cookie jar, knocking down their smaller sibling, taking away a toy, lying through their teeth, or secretly giving their food to the dog. Faulty confession involves a lack of brokenness. There is a vast difference between true brokenness and sorrow for being caught. For a parent, it is the singular goal of Godly discipline to solicit true repentance. This means the child must admit to—and put off—the wrong, and commit to and put on the right (Ephesians 4:17-32). This becomes the essential, foundational template for leading your children to Christ.

The Gospel is to be proclaimed to the simple and to fools.

Simple, foolish—these are stinging words. The Scriptures tell us that *folly is bound up in the heart of a child, but the rod of discipline will drive it far from him* (Proverbs 22:15). Children don't have to be taught to lie, cheat, steal or rebel; it comes to them naturally. That's why Solomon pleas, *"You who are simple, gain prudence; you who are foolish, gain understanding"* (Proverbs 8:5). In this verse, the word *simple* means to be "easily influenced" and *foolish* means to be "intellectually dull and hardened." There it is. Our children are, by nature, intellectually dull (loitering minds!), hardened (prideful!), and easily influenced. Could there be any better definition of a fool?

Like Pharaoh, who hardened his heart when Moses demanded that he release Israel from the bondage of slavery, some children never grow up. During the early plagues that God visited upon Pharaoh, the Scriptures tell us that Pharaoh hardened his heart and refused to release the Hebrew slaves. However, there is a dramatic twist:

Then the Lord said to Moses, "Go to Pharaoh, for I have hardened his heart and the hearts of his officials so that I may perform these miraculous signs of mine among them that you may tell your children and grandchildren how I dealt harshly with the Egyptians and how I performed my signs among them, and that you may know that I am the Lord." So Moses and Aaron went to Pharaoh and said to him, "This is what the Lord, the God of the Hebrews, says: 'How long will you refuse to humble yourself before me? Let my people go, so that they may worship me.'" (Exodus 10:1-3)

Did you catch that? God takes full credit for hardening Pharaoh's heart. Pharaoh, in his sinful stubbornness, crossed a line of no return. Thus, God delivered him over to a reprobate (immoral and unprincipled) mind. He remained hardened in his sin and the rest of the story is history.

Teach your children this story. Read aloud to them the story of the Exodus, for it is the glorious picture of our salvation. In it, we see the Passover feast that is the type of Christ who became our Passover Lamb, and we see Moses, the deliverer, who is the type of Christ, *our* deliverer. We see the destruction of Pharaoh's army as a type of the defeat of Satan, who once enslaved us and our children. And we are given the Ten Commandments, written on tablets of stone, that must be inscribed on our hearts of flesh.

Our children are born hardened and foolish and it is only by the Grace of God that that hardened heart can be changed. Along the way, God may cause them to experience great pain in order to soften their hearts, *because the Lord disciplines those he loves, and he punishes everyone he accepts as a son* (Hebrews 12:6). In Grace, He reaches out to our children and calls them to His Promised Land, eternal Glory. It is Christ who confronts the enemy of our soul, Satan, and demands of him that he let God's children go. He summons the Evil One to the cross, where He crushes Satan's head. He forces him to enter the tomb to show him that it is empty, and that even death could not contain Him. So, let there be no doubt that Christ does indeed *break the power of canceled sin and sets the prisoner free. His blood can make the foulest clean. His blood availed for me.* He is more powerful than any child's hardened heart, and, having earned the right, is worthy to rule as Lord in that child's heart.

Proverbs 22:6 tells us to *Train a child in the way he should go, and when he is old he will not turn from it.* While most are familiar with this verse, few realize that its words are a two-edged sword. This verse promises that if a child is trained and pruned, much like a vine, he will blossom and bear much fruit. Contrariwise, if a child is trained along his natural bent of pride, foolishness and rebellion, when he is older he will not turn from it. The way of life or the way of death hangs in the balance. This innate foolishness *must* be driven out if he is to learn the fear of God; otherwise, he or she will go through life too proud to truly understand and acknowledge their great need for God's saving Grace.

As we continue our journey through Proverbs 8, we next see the picture of a father practically begging his son to heed his words:

"Listen, for I have worthy things to say; I open my lips to speak what is right." (Proverbs 8:6)

This plea comes from a parent who not only understands the consequences of allowing his child to continue in his simple and foolish ways, but a parent who also wants his child to learn how to apply the Wisdom of God. Interestingly enough, the word *worthy* in the above verse means "that pertaining to a prince." The context here is one of a deeply concerned father conveying Wisdom and knowledge to his son, but his words aren't simply idle chatter or casual conversation. He is speaking words that carry the weight and authority of a royal proclamation. It is the image of a very wise king addressing an obedient subject and the message is to be seriously received and acted upon. God so highly values our sons and daughters that He wants us, as parents, to be certain that this "royal heritage" we hold does not become a lost treasure for the lack of Godly guidance.

This dad, who loves his son as a king would love his prince, continues....

"My mouth speaks what is true, for my lips detest wickedness. All the words of my mouth are just; none of them is crooked or perverse." (Proverbs 8:7-8)

Truth is truth. What is true cannot also be false. God's truth never changes, since He alone is truth. *Jesus said, "I am the way and the truth and the life. No one comes to the Father except through me"* (John 14:6). Christ is truth even when our culture's economy, political leaders, philosophies and moral values are constantly changing. The truth of the Gospel is forever constant, an anchor that eternally holds fast. We *must* bring our children to the point of taking a firm hold of it and never letting go.

Jesus Christ is the same yesterday and today and forever (Hebrews 13:8), the incarnate Word of God. When He physically left this world and ascended into heaven, He sent His Holy Spirit who breathed that Word into His apostles, who then penned what the Spirit breathed into them. With the Scriptures as our sure foundation, our children will be able to see that they must choose between two distinctly different value systems in this life—that of the Spirit of Christ, or that of the spirit of Anti-Christ...

"Choose my instruction instead of silver, knowledge rather than choice gold, for wisdom is more precious than rubies, and nothing you desire can compare with her." (Proverbs 8:10-11)

Many years ago, I served in my first pastorate at a large church in Philadelphia, Pennsylvania. The church was spiritually dead, and in the words of one of the members, "the hearse was backed up to the door."

I was 21 at the time, and had only been a Christian for a couple of years. Shortly after I preached my first sermon, I decided to venture down into the dank, musty basement of the massive, cathedral-type building. After some digging around, I came across an old picture of a men's Sunday school class taken just one generation before. As I stood there and counted all the faces in the photograph, I was amazed to realize that there were *over 400 men* in that one class! Four hundred men, sitting under Godly instruction and taking that salt and light back out into their families and neighborhoods to become a redemptive presence for Christ! And I also knew that, within a two-mile radius of that church, there were forty-two other churches with similar old "family portraits." But what quickly shattered my enthusiasm was the realization that all of those churches (mine included) were, for all intents and purposes, now spiritually dead.

Just a few decades after all of those packed, thriving churches, it's safe to say that, for the most part, those days are long gone. Our nation as a whole has become nominal in our Christian faith at best. From Philadelphia to Los Angeles, it has taken only one generation to empty out hundreds of churches in cities throughout the land. America has sadly followed in the footsteps of European countries like England, France, Germany and Switzerland, where cathedrals that once rang out with choruses of worship now rise out of the cities as cold, stone monuments to what used to be. What happened?

We have become more concerned with the balance of our stock portfolios or the value of our homes than with the task of passing down a Godly legacy to the next generation. The love of money, the root of all evil, has gripped the nation and tragically, that includes the Church. Our kids see this and develop a possession-oriented lifestyle of their own. That's why Proverbs 8:10 tells us to *"Choose my instruction instead of silver and knowledge rather than choice gold."* Why? Because *"Wisdom is more precious than rubies, and nothing you desire can compare to her."* There are not enough houses, cars, boats, vacations, clothing or jewelry to compare to the riches that we have in Christ. We must not be so wrapped up with managing our 401(k) that we fail to wrap ourselves in the truth of God's Word. This attitude of neglect and misplaced priorities is what will threaten our spiritual legacy for generations to come. This is what will destroy family faith.

In many countries around the world, Christians are suffering for the Word of God. In places like China and Iran, hundreds of thousands of people die a martyr's death every year. They die unashamedly professing the truth of the Gospel message. This harsh fact should force us to take a hard, honest look at ourselves and ask several questions:

Would we be willing to die for the Gospel like our perse-cuted brethren? Would we be willing to suffer real persecu-tion in order to preserve and protect the integrity of Scrip-ture and insure that its treasures are safely passed on to our heritage? Just how important is God's Word to us, and is it important enough to die for? Persecuted believers throughout history thought so.

Most parents would willingly die for their children, and most would be willing to die for their spouses. But would we *really* be willing to lay down our lives for the sake of the Gospel, when many of us have not even both-ered to share that same Gospel with the family next door, or our kids at home? May God give us an undying love for the Gospel, the Grand Canyon of God's Grace and Mercy.

Teaching Moments

Bible stories are among the most effective means by which you can drive home to your child the importance of acknowledging guilt. Reinforce this principle with these examples from the Scriptures:

• The story of Joseph and his brothers in the book of Genesis, particularly Genesis 42, when Joseph's brothers admitted to one another that, after having sold Joseph into slavery years earlier...

"Surely we are being punished because of our brother. We saw how distressed he was when he pleaded with us for his life, but we would not listen; that's why this distress has come upon us" (Genesis 42:21).

Explain to your child the importance of Joseph's brothers finally acknowledging their guilt in the sin they committed against Joseph.

- The story of Ezra who, with awe-filled grief, prayed before God and acknowledged the Israelites' sin of commingling with the unholy, neighboring people around them...

"O my God, I am too ashamed and disgraced to lift up my face to you, my God, because our sins are higher than our heads and our guilt has reached to the heavens." (Ezra 9:6)

- Trace your own Spiritual Birth Line. Try to identify the "scorch marks" in your life that God used to draw you to the cross. Explain them to your children, if age appropriate, so that they might be able to see how God drew you to Himself. You may want to listen to my sermon series (12 CDs) on the theology behind the Birth Line. (They are available at www.markinc.org)

- Study Ephesians 4:17-32. Note how Paul addresses the two-fold process of change as he speaks of the need to "put off" and to "put on." Identify your child's struggles and map out a plan, including a code of conduct, for putting off ungodly behavior and for putting on the opposite Godly quality. Be sure to spell out both the consequences and the rewards. Identify only one or two issues at a time so as not to exasperate your children.

CHAPTER EIGHT
The Octagonal Gospel

Teach Your Children This Story

MY WIFE, SHARON, wrote this story...

Chuck and I have joined the autumn ritual of cheering on our grandchildren as they run up and down the soccer fields, each one displaying their unique personalities in the way they chased the soccer ball and interacted with teammates. Our son-in-law coached from the sidelines with these words to his five year old twins, "This is the one place you don't have to share! You get to keep the ball all to yourself. If someone tries to take it away from you, don't stand back and say, 'OK, you can have it!'" How do you teach sweet little ones that they must be selfish on the field?

Inner conflicting emotions vied for first place when I saw eight year old Benjamin in his soccer attire, running out onto the field. Benjamin physically resembles Mark and his job as goalie reminded me of Mark's goal tending career. Mark is our youngest and went home to be with Jesus in 1993 at the age of sixteen. Cheering on the outside, I privately pulled up the family videos archived in my heart. I smiled at the scenes of our little guys running the beehive play–the one where every child on the field hovers around the soccer ball. As Chuck and I yelled encouragement from the sidelines, I quickly moved on to vignettes of Mark's growing sports prowess.

Mark was good at every sport he tried but sometimes his mind played tricks on his natural ability. His Little League coaches depended on his big bat for homeruns based on the first few games of hitting homeruns. Then something inside would freeze his confidence and strikeouts reigned. As an athlete himself, Chuck knew the only thing standing between his son and good solid hits was a mental block. I can replay in my mind's eye Chuck standing behind the backstop at home plate. He quietly talked Mark through each time at bat, giving calm step by step reminders of how to do what Mark already knew how to do. I held my breath with each swing and cheered wildly when Mark got on base or hit a homerun. Mark was known in his soccer league as a great goalie. He had what his teammates called the big foot! He could kick a soccer ball fifty yards when he was only twelve. So when he took up football, his coach assigned him all kicking duties in addition to being a wide-receiver. Everyone knew Mark's kicking ability could control field position and thus made winning a lot easier.

Much to everyone's dismay, Mark froze up toward the end of the season. The pressure to perform was too much and once again, a mental block stood between him and victory. At Mark's request, Chuck coached him every evening in the backyard, examining his performance and then patiently counting out his cadence, "Left, right, left, kick!" Every time Mark listened, the ball soared and a big grin turned his anxious face into one of relief and hope.

The football season ended with Mark's team in the championship game, preceded by a pass, punt, and kick competition. Mark's "Big Foot" made him the favored to win the event as he represented his team. As we stood on the sidelines, Mark's face revealed his fear and we watched his body freeze. *What to do? We quickly realized that he could not kick the ball successfully without his dad's help. We didn't want to embarrass him by calling out the necessary encouragement he needed. Mark practiced a few runs toward the ball, each time stopping short. He glanced our way but in his typical reticent manner, he did not ask for help. How could a 12-year-old boy embarrass himself by asking Daddy for help?*

Mark's first two attempts in the contest were disappointing. His teammates and coaches held their breath as Mark set up for his third run at the ball. I prayed, "Lord, please, energize that Big Foot!" I didn't care if he won. I simply wanted him to do what he was able. Without looking at his father, Mark quietly asked, "Dad, count for me." Without a second's hesitation Chuck called out cadence, keeping time with Mark's run toward the ball. Boom, the football soared into the air. Mark's face broke into a thousand little smiles and the fans yelled as his teammates rushed toward our son, knowing he had just won the kicking contest.

Sometimes we need a little help from our Daddy, but He knows it's best to wait until we know our need and we're ready to receive assistance. That morning Mark taught me the value of humility, of admitting my need to the One who is always ready to count for me, to whisper step-by-step instructions in my ear and to cheer me on to victory that is sure to come when I listen to Him.

I'm so glad Mark asked his Daddy to count for him.

This story underscores a critical dimension in successful child-rearing–our children cannot, in their own strength, legitimately come to know Christ. They need their "Daddy" to come alongside them and count out the cadence of the true Gospel message. They will not "get it" until they come to the end of themselves and ask Christ for help. They may make a few meager efforts at turning over a new leaf along the way, but they will always come up short unless or until they cry out, "Father, count for me." The old leaf must be transformed into a new leaf since, as Paul writes, *"Therefore, if anyone is in Christ, he is a new creation; the old has gone, the new has come!"* (2 Corinthians 5:17)

Allow me to explain.

Parenting Principle: Teach your children the character and nature of true salvation.

"I, wisdom, dwell together with prudence; I possess knowledge and discretion. To fear the Lord is to hate evil; I hate pride and arrogance, evil behavior and perverse speech. Counsel and sound judgment are mine; I have understanding and power. By me kings reign and rulers make laws that are just; by me princes govern, and all nobles who rule on earth. I love those who love me, and those who seek me find me. With me are riches and honor, enduring wealth and prosperity. My fruit is better than fine gold; what I yield surpasses choice silver. I walk in the way of righteousness, along the paths of justice, bestowing wealth on those who love me and making their treasuries full. The Lord brought me forth as the first of his works, before his deeds of old; I was appointed from eternity, from the beginning, before the world began. When there were no oceans, I was given birth, when there were no springs abounding with water; before the mountains were settled in place, before the hills, I was given birth, before he made the earth or its fields or any of the dust of the world. I was there when he set the heavens in place, when he marked out the horizon on the face of the deep, when he established the clouds above and fixed securely the fountains of the deep, when he gave the sea its boundary so the waters would not overstep his command, and when he marked out the foundations of the earth. Then I was the craftsman at his side. I was filled with delight day after day, rejoicing always in his presence, rejoicing in his whole world and delighting in mankind.

Now then, my sons, listen to me; blessed are those who keep my ways. Listen to my instruction and be wise; do not ignore it. Blessed is the man who listens to me, watching daily at my doors, waiting at my doorway. For whoever finds me finds life and receives favor from the Lord. But whoever fails to find me harms himself; all who hate me love death."
Proverbs 8:12-36

The dream begins when you and your spouse learn that a child, a precious gift from God, is on the way. Long before the child's anticipated arrival you frequent the local department stores to stock up on clothing, baby furniture, and cartons of diapers. As the months pass, you stay busy painting the spare bedroom, reading parenting books and magazines, and talking with family and friends about how your life will change once the baby arrives.

Along the way, the anticipation builds. You spend hours dreaming about this unborn child and thinking about all the hopes and plans you have for his future. Who will this child be? What kind of a man or woman will he or she become once they are born into this world? Will he become a renowned scientist or an inconspicuous office clerk? Will she be a president or a lab technician? Will they be healthy?

Did you know that God also has a dream for your child? He reveals that dream in pieces, like puzzle-parts, as the mosaic comes together. He will use events, circumstances, relatives, friends, the Church—and most of all, many varied crises along the way—to crystallize that dream. But the fullness of God's dream for your child will never be realized apart from the Gospel. It is through that true Gospel—faithfully imparted, unfettered by human will, intellect, or emotion—that a child comes to faith in Christ. God has no grandchildren, just children.

Yet to all who received him, to those who believed in his name, he gave the right to become children of God— children born not of natural descent, nor of human decision or a husband's will, but born of God. (John 1:12-13)

In the last chapter, we discussed certain facets of the Gospel message that your children must learn. As we continue our journey through Proverbs 8, we next discover that verses 12-36 contain eight core attributes of the true Gospel, or what I like to call "The Octagonal Gospel."

Attribute #1: The true Gospel is a practical Gospel.

"I, wisdom, dwell together with prudence;
I possess knowledge and discretion."
Proverbs 8:12

Since this book is practical by design, I will go into more detail on this first attribute as we move further along in this chapter. By definition, the word *prudence* in the above verse means "to practically deal with the daily issues of life." It also carries the dictionary definition of "showing carefulness and foresight."

This means that your children must come to understand that the Bible and the Gospel message it contains is not merely ethereal and subjective, with no real practical value, but that it represents an objective faith with real answers to the real questions that children will inevitably ask. As the challenges they face in life intensify, the Gospel will become more and more practical and relevant and tailored to their needs by the Holy Spirit. The Gospel of Jesus Christ can be applied to any situation, circumstance or relational problem you could possibly imagine.

Your children must discover that there is no book, tape, CD, or human counselor that is a better resource than the Word of God itself. The Bible is the story of God's plan of redemption, from creation and the curse upon Satan in

Genesis 3:15, to the final consummation in the book of Revelation. It is the story of how the "seed of the woman" crushed the head of Satan, a story of spiritual warfare down through the generations. And the battle ground is the soul of your child.

That being said, we must remember that, although it is intense spiritual warfare, it is not really a fair fight. The story of redemption is not about two *equally* strong foes battling against each other with the outcome of that struggle being in doubt. The victory has already been won when Christ conquered sin and death. Notice how the curse upon the devil is worded...

"And I will put enmity between you and the woman, and between your offspring and hers; he will crush your head, and you will strike his heel." (Genesis 3:15)

There it is–the outcome of the war could not be clearer. The "Seed of the Woman" (Christ) will crush the head of Satan. And in the process, Satan will *strike* his heel (i.e., the crucifixion). That same power that won the battle for the soul of your child promises to indwell them in their life-long struggle against the flesh, that is, against the damage that was done to their mind, will, and intellect as descendants of Adam. The good news is that, if they have trusted Christ, their final sanctification is also a done deal in the heart and mind of God. This is why the Gospel is so practical–God is preparing us for Glory. And since no sin can enter heaven, the cleansing work begins when your child trusts Christ, and will end when he or she is glorified in His presence.

Sanctification (to set apart as sacred or Holy) is the work of the Holy Spirit as our Counselor, our Advocate.

"If you love me, you will obey what I command. And I will ask the Father, and he will give you another Counselor to be with you forever—the Spirit of truth. The world cannot

accept him, because it neither sees him nor knows him. But you know him, for he lives with you and will be in you." (John 14:15-17)

That word *Counselor* literally means "to come alongside." It is the picture of our Father standing beside us and counting the cadence of life, instructing us on how to succeed. When Wisdom (i.e., Jesus Christ) dwells together with prudence (Proverbs 8:12), they hold in their hands God's own sacred and practical recipe for successful life management. Jesus Christ is not merely some intangible, fabled storybook character, but a living Savior who became flesh, dwelt amongst us, and promises to indwell all who trust Him.

Paul raises, and answers, this thought-provoking question:

For who has known the mind of the Lord that he may instruct him? But we have the mind of Christ. (1 Corinthians 2:16)

We have the mind of Christ! Can there be anything more practical and uplifting than that? To know Christ is to possess His mind, the Wisdom of God. If our children don't know Christ, they will not be able to understand the Scriptures. And if they do not know the Scriptures they can never know His mind.

The man without the Spirit does not accept the things that come from the Spirit of God, for they are foolishness to him, and he cannot understand them, because they are spiritually discerned. The spiritual man makes judgments about all things. (1 Corinthians 2:14-15a)

God's dream for your child is a costly one—the death of His Son on the cross. One proof or evidence that the Gospel has crystallized in your child's heart is when they begin to ask themselves this question: *How, as the mind of Christ is revealed to me, am I going to understand God's dream for my life?*

The book of Hebrews tells us...

Therefore, since we have a great high priest who has gone through the heavens, Jesus the Son of God, let us hold firmly to the faith we profess. For we do not have a high priest who is unable to sympathize with our weaknesses, but we have one who has been tempted in every way, just as we are—yet without sin. Let us then approach the throne of grace with confidence, so that we may receive mercy and find grace to help us in our time of need. (Hebrews 4:14-16)

What does this passage mean? It means that your children should know they have the mind of Christ while facing any of life's disheartening challenges—when they're:

- afraid;
- in pain;
- under pressure or temptation;
- lonely or confused;
- discouraged by multiple failures.

Never let them forget that the God they serve has gone through every situation or temptation they themselves will ever face. He is our High Priest who makes intercession for us even when we do not know how to pray...

In the same way, the Spirit helps us in our weakness. We do not know what we ought to pray for, but the Spirit himself intercedes for us with groans that words cannot express. And he who searches our hearts knows the mind of the Spirit, because the Spirit intercedes for the saints in accordance with God's will. (Romans 8:26-27)

Attribute #2: The centerpiece of the true Gospel is the Holiness of God.

Is there such a thing as evil? The answer may seem obvious. In fact, this is the very question two United States presidential candidates were asked at a religious forum on national television during the 2008 election. Why would such a question even need to be asked? Because the definition of evil has become blurred as our culture has succumbed to the moral relativists, humanists and secular media elite. Our children are in dire danger of being sacrificed on the altars of their high priests and priestesses—the rock stars, movie stars, advertisers and educators.

Their so-called "god of love," if they accept God's existence at all, is a tolerant god who winks at every form of human depravity. Yet, the God of the Bible *hates*. Did you know that? Our God hates—He hates sin. His holiness demands that He cannot even look upon sin, and He will *never* compromise with it. That's why we read in the book of Proverbs...

To fear the Lord is to hate evil; "I hate pride and arrogance, evil behavior and perverse speech." (Proverbs 8:13)

An even greater source of ridicule, on the part of certain elements in our modern culture, is the Biblical reality that evil has an intelligent, scheming personification—namely, Satan. Pervasive evil exists in the world today because, even before the world was created, God's Holiness would not permit even rebellious angels to remain in His presence. Since their expulsion from heaven, the Evil One roams the earth with his cohorts, *seeking whom he may devour* (1 Peter 5:8). Cartoonish caricatures and "rational denial" are aimed at desensitizing your children about both the very existence and intentions of Satan, as well as God's eternal holiness.

God hated evil enough to send His only Son to die on Calvary's cross, and to nail each and every one of our sins to the cross with Him in the process. Think about it for a moment. God the Father turned His back on His Son amidst His screams of *"My God, my God, why have you forsaken me?"* (Mark 15:34) In the courts of heaven, there were twelve legions of angels waiting for a nod from the Father to deliver Christ from that cross! (Matthew 26:53) Yet, the Father turned His back because He will not look upon sin—He *hates* sin. His holiness demands it. Despite what peer pressure and the world around them are saying, your children should understand that evil is a very real thing, and God hates it.

Attribute #3: One who is genuinely saved will be tested.

In the next verse of Proverbs 8, God says ...

"Counsel and sound judgment are mine; I have understanding and power." (Proverbs 8:14)

Did you catch these words? *Counsel, sound judgment, understanding, power.*

Compare these words with what Paul said to the Corinthian congregation...

No temptation has seized you except what is common to man. And God is faithful; he will not let you be tempted beyond what you can bear. But when you are tempted, he will also provide a way out so that you can stand up under it. (1 Corinthians 10:13)

The Christian life is hard when it is lived out correctly. At times, it involves pain, suffering and heartache, and requires perseverance, discipline and faithfulness through trials. The Scriptures never promise us that God will remove these things from our lives—in fact, God says just the opposite by telling us to stand up under it. Although He will never subject us to more than we are able to bear, God often allows us to go through the fire so that we might feel and experience the same temptations He felt, and in the process, step out in faith and trust that we are always in His sure and steady grip.

Against the backdrop of imminent suffering, the early Church was challenged to suffer and stand up with grace and dignity. They needed *counsel, sound judgment, understanding, and power.* The persecutions, for the most part (with some exceptions), were not widespread, but rather localized. Rome viewed the early Christians as merely another sect of Judaism and dealt with them on a case-by-case or city-by-city basis.

The early persecutions, from the time of Emperor Trajan (A.D. 111) through most of the second and third centuries, allowed that a Roman citizen bring any charge at any time against their Christian neighbor. False charges were common. A Christian only had to look at his neighbor cross-eyed and a trial would be held and the believer ordered to recant his faith. If he recanted he was set free. Countless numbers of Christians refused to deny their Lord and were tortured until they did, or were martyred using any one of the many gruesome Roman execution methods available at the time. In that context Peter says:

But how is it to your credit if you receive a beating for doing wrong and endure it? But if you suffer for doing good and you endure it, this is commendable before God. To this you were called, because Christ suffered for you, leaving you an example that you should follow in his steps. (1 Peter 2:20-21)

There are times in our lives when the pressure seems too great. It certainly seemed to us that God had "crossed the line" when we were left to bear the agony of our young son's death. In the days and weeks after losing Mark, I remember praying, *God, I can't bear up under this...You can't take something that I love this much away from me. I can't bear to watch my wife, my sons and my daughter in this much pain.* I felt forsaken by God.

Years later, I'm now able to say that the same God who had seemingly gone too far is still in the process of gently redeeming the pain of that loss. We still miss our son and always will. There is no such thing as closure. One learns to adjust to redefine what it means to be normal. Yet, we can say our God is sovereign and we can trust Him with our lives and especially the lives of our children.

Throughout the early years of our grief, God gave us *counsel, sound judgment, understanding, and power.* He did this by driving us to His written Word. There were times when the Scripture and hymns seemed to mock us in our pain. To us, each one of the following verses is a story unto itself when our hope was fading.

"I will give you the treasures of darkness, riches stored in secret places, so that you may know that I am the Lord, the God of Israel, who summons you by name." (Isaiah 45:3)

"I will repay you for the years the locusts have eaten—the great locust and the young locust, the other locusts and the locust swarm—my great army that I sent among you." (Joel 2:25)

God gave the former verse to my wife and the latter to me in the throes of great sorrow, and we have rested upon these promises. Truly, the Scriptures are what give us *counsel, sound judgment, understanding, and power.*

Attribute #4: Christ is sovereign and He can be trusted.

The world is a troubling place. News of the mounting woes of a global economy, rising poverty, terrorism and unending wars and rumors of war have become a daily diet for us and our children. In the most critical moments of Jesus' post-resurrection appearances, when the disciples were afraid, troubled and in hiding, His first words to them were, *"Do not be afraid!"* His glorious plan of salvation was fixed from eternity with precision and detail. Every star, planet, constellation, moon and galaxy was created with purpose and order. It is this same God who fashioned the world with just a word and is in absolute control over the destinies of men and nations.

Take a look at a very interesting dialogue between Jesus and His disciples...

Jesus left the temple and was walking away when his disciples came up to him to call his attention to its buildings. "Do you see all these things?" he asked. "I tell you the truth, not one stone here will be left on another; every one will be thrown down." As Jesus was sitting on the Mount of Olives, the disciples came to him privately. "Tell us," they said, "when will this happen, and what will be the sign of your coming and of the end of the age?" Jesus answered: "Watch out that no one deceives you. For many will come in my name, claiming, 'I am the Christ,' and will deceive many. You will hear of wars and rumors of wars, but see to it that you are not alarmed. Such things must happen, but the end is still to come. Nation will rise against nation, and kingdom against kingdom. There will be famines and earthquakes in various places. All these are the beginning of birth pains." (Matthew 24:1-8)

Birth pains? Imagine an expectant mother who is about to go into natural labor. As her water breaks and the contractions start, she quickly realizes that it is only a matter of moments before she will have to endure the most intensely painful experience of her life—and there's nothing at all that she can do to stop it. Although she doesn't know exactly when the experience will end, she *does* know that great joy will come at the end of the birthing process.

This is the analogy Jesus is using in the words of these verses. Although the world seems to be spinning out of control all around us, He has told us that we have no reason to be alarmed because we serve a God who is always in control over the laws of nature and the affairs of men. In the book of Proverbs, God reminds us that...

"By me kings reign and rulers make laws that are just; by me princes govern, and all nobles who rule on earth." (Proverbs 8:15-16)

Since the beginning of history—from Greece to Rome, from the Caesars to the Ayatollahs, from Babylon to Persia, from the Soviet Union to Iraq, from Great Britain to America, world leaders, drunk with power, believed *they* were sovereign. What they failed to understand is that *God* is the One Who is in true control of world governments and kingdoms, no matter who occupies the man-made seats of power. But unlike these prideful yet foolish leaders, our children must understand that God is *always* sovereign, even when world events and circumstances become overwhelmingly frightening.

Attribute #5: Our salvation originates with God and not us.

This is an especially critical component of the saving Gospel and one that our children *must* come to understand. In Europe and the rest of the West, over the past 100 years or so, the Church has lost her understanding of the "Doctrines of Grace." Massive cathedrals with rich histories now stand empty throughout Europe as the God of the Bible has been gradually abandoned—and America is not far behind. Evangelicals are now in a distinct minority, despite our being often (but wrongly) referred to as a Christian nation.

Sadly, we still tend to think that our good works determine our salvation—that if we become worthy in God's sight simply by being good enough, we will earn our ticket to heaven. However, this is not at all the true Gospel as laid out in the Bible. Our salvation is, in fact, God-initiated.

"I love those who love me, and those who seek me find me" (Proverbs 8:17).

At first glance, one might think Solomon is placing a condition on God's love, as if God is saying, *"If* you love me, *then* I will love you in return." But such is not the case. It is *because* of God's love that we are *enabled* to experience that love, and then to love Him in return. We seek Him only because He sought us first.

This is love: not that we loved God, but that he loved us and sent his Son as an atoning sacrifice for our sins. (1 John 4:10)

For he chose us in him before the creation of the world to be Holy and blameless in his sight. (Ephesians 1:4)

But we ought always to thank God for you, brothers loved by the Lord, because from the beginning God chose you to be saved through the sanctifying work of the Spirit and through belief in the truth. He called you to this through our Gospel, that you might share in the glory of our Lord Jesus Christ. (2 Thessalonians 2:13-14)

"You did not choose me, but I chose you and appointed you to go and bear fruit—fruit that will last." (John 15:16)

Our search for God begins when He regenerates, or brings back to life, the wicked and depraved heart that exists in each of us. He then creates within us a desire to know Him and even gives us faith to believe. God and God alone can bring a dead soul back to life so that we might have the ability and desire to repent and believe. We do not seek after God by nature; our nature must first be changed by His loving Grace before we will seek after God. It is God's incredible love for us that drives His Grace, and not our feeble human efforts or works.

That's why the book of Jeremiah tells us...

The Lord appeared to us in the past, saying: "I have loved you with an everlasting love; I have drawn you with loving-kindness." (Jeremiah 31:3)

It's a good thing God initiates our salvation, isn't it? If *my* salvation depended on me, my day-to-day emotions, or my good deeds, I would be saved today and lost tomorrow. By offering up a lifetime of our good works, we cannot possibly manage to earn God's salvation for even a single day. All of our good works simply add up to a pile of *filthy rags* (Isaiah 64:6). Since God's salvation requires that we be perfect (Matthew 5:48), and none of us qualify (Romans 3:23), we need a Savior. Yes, it is a marvelous thing that God Himself does the initiating.

Attribute #6: The Gospel promises an unparalleled inheritance.

How do you measure wealth? Are you wealthy with a million dollars? Ten million? What if you owned a 20,000 square foot mansion, with seven exotic cars—one for each day of the week—sparkling gloriously in the garage? Exactly how much would you need to be satisfied that you are *wealthy*? How much would be enough for you?

What is lasting wealth? Wisdom (Christ) calls out to us from Proverbs 8...

"With me are riches and honor, enduring wealth and prosperity. My fruit is better than fine gold; what I yield surpasses choice silver. I walk in the way of righteousness, along the paths of justice, bestowing wealth on those who love me and making their treasuries full." (Proverbs 8:18-21)

Only those found in Christ through repentance and faith can claim these riches as their own. Unlike anything else we possess, these treasures are eternal. Our kids need to be motivated by a different definition of wealth—the glorious prosperity that awaits us in our spiritual inheritance in Christ. And, whatever we must endure in this sinful, fallen world will dissipate in the afterglow of His wondrous Glory that will soon be revealed to us. Our children must understand that this earthly life is *not* all there is, and that, as believers, we have true and lasting treasures already stored up for us—not just for a few months or years, but for all eternity. Let this be your doxology to your children...

Praise be to the God and Father of our Lord Jesus Christ! In his great mercy he has given us new birth into a living hope through the resurrection of Jesus Christ from the dead, and into an inheritance that can never perish, spoil or fade—kept in heaven for you, who through faith are shielded by God's power until the coming of the salvation that is ready to be revealed in the last time. (1 Peter 1:4-5)

Attribute #7: Christ is God, the Creator of the universe.

Most Christian parents introduce the story of Creation with picture books, devotionals, or even DVDs and videos, used as guides to help them illustrate for their children God's incredible power and love as He spoke the entire universe into existence. But have you taught them about what came *before* Creation?

"The Lord brought me forth as the first of his works, before his deeds of old; I was appointed from eternity, from the beginning, before the world began. When there were no oceans, I was given birth, when there were no springs abounding with water; before the mountains were settled in place, before the hills, I was given birth, before he made the earth or its fields or any of the dust of the world. I was there when he set the heavens in place, when he marked out the horizon on the face of the deep, when he established the clouds above and fixed securely the fountains of the deep, when he gave the sea its boundary so the waters would not overstep his command, and when he marked out the foundations of the earth. Then I was the craftsman at his side. I was filled with delight day after day, rejoicing always in his presence, rejoicing in his whole world and delighting in mankind." (Proverbs 8:22-31)

Wisdom speaks. And what does He say? That Jesus, our wonderful Savior, the Wisdom of God was in the very beginning with God the Father as the agent of creation. He has no beginning and He has no end, for He was *appointed before eternity.* He didn't first appear on the scene as a newborn baby in a manger some 2,000 plus years ago; Christ existed *before* the creation of the world in the mystery of His Godhead. He was the architect and craftsman at His Father's side, and even as the earth was being fashioned, He was *delighting in mankind.*

In speaking of Christ, Paul said:

He (Christ) is the image of the invisible God, the firstborn over all creation. For by him all things were created: things in heaven and on earth, visible and invisible, whether thrones or powers or rulers or authorities; all things were created by him and for him. He is before all things, and in him all things hold together. And he is the head of the body, the church; he is the beginning and the firstborn from among the dead, so that in everything he might have the supremacy. (Colossians 1:15-18)

All of those who are truly saved in Christ were delightful visions in the heart and mind of the God who knew them even before the world began. This is an integral part of the Gospel message to be shared with your children—because, although God took pleasure in creating the entire universe and everything in it, His greatest delight is *not* found in heaven, angels, streets of gold, pearly gates, or the great expanse of the universe. God's true delight is in His Church, His people, saved by His blood.

Is that not a wonderful dream for your saved child to cherish?

Attribute #8: The true Gospel involves the choice between two ways and two destinies.

Imagine you're driving down a long, country dirt road. You already know that you took a wrong turn miles back and now you're driving along with high hopes of spotting a sign, *any* sign, that will give you a clue as to where you're going. And then, you come to that dreaded fork in the road. Now which way should you go? If you take one path over the other you could end up even farther away from your desired destination. But which way is the right way, and what will happen if you choose the wrong path instead of the right one?

When it comes to our salvation, the way home is not nearly as mysterious as a fork in the road. But the consequences of taking the wrong turn are severe! God has plainly revealed for us the two paths—and there are only two—

that we can take: one path leads to eternal life and the other leads to death...

"Now then, my sons, listen to me; blessed are those who keep my ways. Listen to my instruction and be wise; do not ignore it. Blessed is the man who listens to me, watching daily at my doors, waiting at my doorway. For whoever finds me finds life and receives favor from the Lord. But whoever fails to find me harms himself; all who hate me love death." (Proverbs 8:32-36)

There it is...two paths, two eternal destinies, clearly laid out for us in the book of Proverbs: to find Christ means life, to not find Christ means death. And it is this unalterable truth, inseparably bound to the uncompromising holiness of God, on which the entire Gospel hinges.

Parents, teach your children the octagonal gospel of Grace.

Teaching Moments

• Make "talk time" a natural part of your child's life. Our son, Chuck, instituted "talk time" with his firstborn child, Markie, as soon as Markie could talk. Every night when Chuck tucked Markie into bed, they reviewed the day together. Chuck had seen so many teenagers grow up with a coldness towards their parents and wondered how it was that these once loving little children could so easily become hardened toward their parents. Chuck started these special moments with simple, childlike questions: "What did you do today? What was the most fun? What was hardest? What happened today that made you sad?" At the end of talk time, Chuck used to say, "Markie, you can tell me anything...if you are sad, you can tell me...if you are confused...I'll help you understand...if you are scared....you can talk to me....I used to be a little child just like you...I will never laugh at you or make you feel badly about yourself...if

I do, I will apologize." As Markie grew older, their conversations took on deeper significance because our grandson knew that he could trust Daddy to help him work through the rough spots of the day, whether it was a bully encounter, a teacher who seemed unfair, or theological questions. Chuck recently said that he knew that whatever upset Markie during the day would come out in this nighttime ritual. Chuck used this time to teach Markie how the many dimensions of a walk with Christ have implications in daily life. Chuck's purpose in this "talk time" was to plant firmly in his son's heart the fact that he could come to Daddy with anything and his dad would help him figure out appropriate responses and proper boundaries. Review the story at the beginning of this chapter and the challenge to teach our children to trust God to "count" for them. Chuck is "counting" for his son in a way that is teaching him how practical the Gospel really is in day-to-day situations. Consider what might be the best part of your day for establishing a "talk time" as a routine for your child.

• Study each of the eight attributes and think about how they apply to specific childhood discipline or teaching moments in your family. Write out the eight attributes of the Gospel on several 3 x 5 cards. Keep one in your Bible that you regularly review during personal study time, post one on your refrigerator, over the kitchen sink and by your computer. When faced with a discipline issue, immediately review these attributes and ask God to show you how they apply to the current situation and how to communicate this truth in a way your child can understand.

• Teach your children how practical the Gospel is by making prayer a natural part of your daily life. From the time our babies could sit up, we folded their hands while we prayed at mealtime and expected them to learn how to listen quietly. Once, on our way to visit friends in the mountains of Pennsylvania, we ran into a sudden ice storm. The further up into the mountains we drove, the more treacherous the roads became. Our two older children, ages nine and eight, understood that we were in a dangerous situation as they watched cars sliding off the road and they could easily see that, if we slid to the left, our car would fall down the side of the mountain. Even the two babies, ages twenty-four months and nine months, seemed to know that they had to be quiet while Daddy tried to keep us all safe. When Heidi asked, "Daddy, what's going to happen?" I responded, "We need to pray." No sooner had we finished asking for God's help when a big sand truck pulled in front of our car. From that point on we drove on a well-sanded highway and arrived safely at our friend's home. The practical lesson of trusting God in the darkness and the daily applications of the Gospel were not lost on our young children that day.

• Find fun ways to teach your children that the message of the Gospel presents a choice between two pathways and two destinies. Shortly after the birth of our son, Mark, Sharon decided that she had had enough of the fighting and grumbling between our two older children, ages nine and seven. She strived to make the evening meal more peaceful but to no avail. One night, she pulled out a pair of old sunglasses that she had decorated with fake eyebrows. She said, "The Bible forbids us to grumble. From now on, if you do not behave at the dinner table, you will put on these glasses, walk around the table and announce, 'I am a rude and ignorant person.'" I thought to myself, "Sharon, don't do this unless you follow through." She continued, "No one *has* to wear these glasses. It's your choice. If you grumble about the food or tease your brother or sister, you are choosing to wear them. If you don't want to wear them, then choose to behave." I won't tell you who chose which pathway, but I will say that my wife followed through and, after some tears, we ended up sharing lots of good laughter together.

• Establish a Code of Conduct. A Code of Conduct helps you identify specific character issues that seem difficult for your child to overcome and establishes types of discipline appropriate for the misconduct. Identify several specific discipline issues for your child, such as lying, talking back, and slow obedience. Create a chart that you will post on your refrigerator or your child's bedroom door. List the obedience issues on the left side of the chart, along with appropriate Scripture. On the right side of the chart, list the discipline that will take place if the child disobeys. Take your child to the chart and calmly explain all of the rules and consequences. Ask them to repeat back to you what you have just described. Then say, "Now, this is a tool to help you remember what Mommy and Daddy want you to learn. It's your choice. We don't have to worry about the discipline because you're going to choose to obey, right? But, just in case you don't obey, then what will happen?"

When your child disobeys, take them to the chart (even children who can't read can understand this process) and ask them to tell you what the chart says. Explain that you must discipline them because they made the choice to disobey.

Don't underestimate your child's ability to understand the attributes of the Gospel. Our daughter shared this story:

"Yesterday, the four youngest kids were driving me nuts. They were constantly chasing each other, yelling, screaming and fighting. So, I sat them all down. They sat for a good 15 minutes, and I looked at them sternly and said, 'Is this fun?' Benny nodded his head and said 'yes.' I said, 'It is?' He replied, 'It means you love us, so it's good when you make us sit.' Danielle looked at him like he was crazy. But he said, 'Don't you remember Granddad told us that parents love their children if they punish them?' (not an exact quote!). 'So, when they make us sit, it means they love us.' Then he gave me a smile that I couldn't resist and I let them get up."

Who says a five-year-old can't grasp the deeper meaning behind your teachings, Dad? Moments like this stay with a child for the rest of their lives...and it's very likely that they'll pass it on.

CHAPTER NINE
Teach Your Children to Love the Church

Teach Your Children This Story

ALL WHO MET Barbara and Howard Weldin loved them. They were quiet and unassuming people, always radiating hope and love with a smile and contagious hardiness-of-soul.

Although the Weldins faithfully attended church each week, they weren't widely known among the members of their large congregation. Barbara's many years of teaching Bible studies earned her the love and respect of younger women who saw her as a spiritual mother. Although neither Howard nor Barbara served in any of the more visible levels of leadership roles in their local church, they did one of the most important things anyone could ever do for their church family: they prayed with fervor.

Even after Barbara died from a fast growing cancer, Howard continued serving his church through prayer. During Sunday morning services, he always sat in the farthest corner of the sanctuary's balcony, listening intently to the sermon and praying quietly for his pastor and the other church leaders. Whoever in the congregation needed hope or a loving touch from God, Howard faithfully prayed for them with earnest perseverance. In good times and bad, day in and day out, Howard could be counted on for prayer, whatever the need.

Sharon knew that Howard prayed regularly for me, so when our son Chuck joined our church staff, Sharon asked Howard and our friend, John Krauss, to add him to their prayer ministry. She knew that Howard and John walked together every morning. These two Godly men used this time not just for exercise, but as a "prayer walk" of intercession for the needs of the church and her people. Each day, rain or shine, hot or cold, they faithfully met and interceded for their pastor, church leaders, and the entire congregation.

When John passed away, the church grieved the loss of this precious prayer warrior. As Howard aged into his eighties without his prayer buddy and was no longer able to walk the way he once used to, he still continued to pray. His faithfulness never wavered throughout the remaining years of his life. We wonder if in God's economy, Howard's most fruitful eternal work took place in the waning years of his life as he impacted thousands of lives through prayer. Howard was physically fragile but spiritually, ever growing, ever young.

When God called Howard home, his funeral was quiet and sparsely attended. Since he had spent so many years in anonymity, few were even aware of his passing. Although they ministered quietly behind the scenes, Howard and Barbara Weldin faithfully lived out a lifetime of service to their Lord and to His people. They did so because *they truly and selflessly loved the Church.*

Parenting Principle: Teach your children to love the Church.

*Wisdom has built her house; she has hewn out
its seven pillars. She has prepared her meat and
mixed her wine; she has also set her table. She has sent
out her maids, and she calls from the highest point of the*

city. "Let all who are simple come in here!" she says to
those who lack judgment. "Come, eat my food and drink
the wine I have mixed. Leave your simple ways and you
will live; walk in the way of understanding."
Proverbs 9:1-6

In their recently released book, *unChristian: What a New Generation Really Thinks About Christianity* (Baker Books, 2007), authors David Kinnaman and Gabe Lyons found that:

> There is an increasingly negative reputation of Christians, especially among young Americans. Christians are best known for what they are against, rather than what they're for.... They are perceived as being judgmental, anti-homosexual, and too political. And, young people are quick to point out that they believe Christianity is no longer as Jesus intended. People have many things to say about the church these days.

We often hear from a variety of critics who say that the Church is too hypocritical, too money-oriented, or not even relevant to today's culture. Young people say that the Church is not cool enough while older people complain that it's *too* cool. Simple men complain that the Church is too difficult to understand while scholars criticize it for being too simple, and still others claim that it's too judgmental. Evangelicals complain that the fundamentalists are too legalistic while fundamentalists point a finger and claim that evangelicals are too liberal.

Churchgoers often drive home from the Sunday morning service complaining that the pastor's sermon was way too long, the music selection was too traditional or too contemporary, or the noisy baby in the back row was too distracting, or...or...or...you get the point. And those are the *nicest* things we say! Yet, when it comes to writing an encouraging note to a church leader, speaking a word of gratitude or lifting them up in regular prayer, we often fall short.

The real tragedy is that all of this happens within earshot of our children. Those who engage in this habit of criticism live with very little regard for how their child's image of the Church is being shaped by such negativity. Despite the fact that our children don't hear us pray for our pastors and church leaders or seldom see us tithe or serve the Church in any capacity, somehow we're still dumbfounded when they become teenagers and "suddenly" have no interest in the Church or its people. And I couldn't begin to recall the number of parents of these lost children who blame "the church" for not holding onto their kids.

Listen carefully. Churches die when we fail to pass on our legacy of faith in Christ and love for His Church. We gradually erode their view of the Church every time we roast the preacher, stir the pot of controversy, or refuse to be introspective. If we want a Godly generation to follow after us in our children we must teach them to *love the Church*. In this chapter, we will look at the three reasons, laid out for us in the ninth chapter of Proverbs, why this principle of loving the Church is so critical to raising children who know, love and fear God. When you own these principles as truth, you will be equipped to pass on to your children the critical priority of loving the Church—and they, in turn, will reflect that love to your grandchildren.

Reason #1: The Church is the bride of Christ and belongs exclusively to Him.

> *Wisdom has built her house...*
> Proverbs 9:1

If you've been reading this book from the very beginning you know by now that, in the Scriptures, Jesus is the personification of Wisdom. So, as we investigate the above verse from Proverbs 9 in its context, we learn that Wisdom (a feminine word in the Hebrew, but with a masculine meaning), that is, Jesus, has built His house. Wisdom is Jesus; He is the bridegroom, we are His bride...and we are the Church that *He* has built.

Throughout history, God has always had a people for Himself. From Noah to Elijah, from the nation of Israel to the disciples who walked with Jesus, this special group of people has endured for generations. And despite their flaws and sinful faults, God's people are still the best people in the world to be around.

The Church has been burned on crosses, devoured by dogs, lions and leopards, and even brought to the brink of extinction during the Middle-Ages. She has survived suppression by Communism, the death camps of Nazism and the clutches of cruel dictators, and she will triumph over the aspirations of Islamic world domination. Since the birth of the Church, she has been ridiculed, scorned, defamed, fragmented, misrepresented, mocked, blasphemed and intimidated. And yet, she has remained as the world's only beacon of hope, holding forth the true light of the Gospel message. The Church has survived the onslaught of evil brought to bear against her, because *Wisdom* (Christ) *has built her house* (the Church).

Not long after Hurricane Ike took its toll on much of the southern United States in September 2008, a remarkable photo was published nationwide of a beachfront home belonging to Pam and Warren Adams in Gilchrist, Texas. Although the hurricane's winds and raging flood waters had decimated every other home around it, the Adams' property was the only one left standing in a landscape of total devastation.

Twelve days before Christmas and three months after Ike destroyed their community, the grateful couple purchased fifty dollars worth of holiday lights and decorated their front porch with the shape of a Christmas tree, illuminated with power from a generator. The lights could be seen by people as far away (by several miles) as Highway

87, along the Bolivar Peninsula, and were described as a glowing beacon in the darkness, evidence that "there is still life in Gilchrist."[1]

The Adams home withstood one of the worst hurricanes in recent history for one simple reason: it was built stronger than all of the other oceanfront homes around it. Likewise, Christ's Church has also been built to a different standard—the atoning blood of Christ—precious, incorruptible and imperishable. Kingdoms rise and fall, nations come and go. Kings and politicians live and die. Even when the storms of war and political disarray come and wipe everything else away, His Church is, and always will be, left standing. And in the end, we *will* win the victory, because our God is sovereign and we can trust Him.

We must view the Church through the grid of God's values, not the limitations of human sinfulness. In the early 80's, Sharon and I went through four years of incredible pain and disappointment in a church we loved (and still do), among people with whom we had labored for ten years. We saw the good, the bad, and the ugly. But for the last four years of our tenure there we saw mostly the ugly. During those times of disillusionment I often considered leaving the ministry. I rationalized that I did not need this, I did not deserve this, and I could no longer endure the level of disrespect and mean-spiritedness we were experiencing. Over the years, I have often said that I needed to quit the ministry and get into something safe like sky-diving! We paid a heavy price with health issues and emotional heartache that took years to heal, leaving many scars on our souls.

The individual circumstances of those four years constitute a drama unto themselves. Even as I write, my soul wells up with tears. But, we were to be unwilling players in a far more tragic drama yet to come. Seven years after we resigned from that church, we lost our sixteen-year-old son, Mark, in a devastating car accident. His death made the pain of those four years of church conflict pale by comparison.

Our children ranged in age from elementary school to teenagers during that church crisis. One of our parenting values is that we would not place adult-sized burdens on our children. So, in this situation, our top priority was to protect them from the ugliness of church politics. We wanted our children to always see the church as their second home and the church family as a safe haven. Our desire was to protect them from becoming victims of the fallout that occurs in so many pastoral families where kids grow to hate the Church because of the pain they see the ministry often causes. When we were tempted to throw in the towel, to give up on our calling, God reminded us that the Church is still the bride of Christ, and that in spite of the imperfections of God's people (including us!) we had to teach our children to love Her, to support Her, to be loyal to Her, and to protect Her witness. Our children also needed to understand that the Church is a hospital for sinners, not a museum of "saints." However, this is not a license for people to lose control of their basest internal instincts as we are so prone to do in the process of resolving local church conflicts.

In Ephesians chapter 5, the Apostle Paul gives some pertinent instructions concerning the husband–wife relationship. In so doing, he compares that relationship to the one between Christ and His bride–the Church...

Submit to one another out of reverence for Christ. Wives, submit to your husbands as to the Lord, for the husband is the head of the wife as Christ is the head of the church, his body, of which he is the Savior. Now as the church submits to Christ, so also wives should submit to their husbands in everything. Husbands, love your wives, just as Christ loved the church and gave himself up for her to make her Holy, cleansing her by the washing with water through the word, and to present her to himself as a radiant church, without stain or wrinkle or any other blemish, but Holy and blameless. In this same way, husbands ought to love their wives as their own bodies. He who loves his wife loves himself. After all, no one ever hated his own body, but he feeds and cares for it, just as Christ does the church—for we are members of his body. "For this reason a man will leave his father and mother and be united to his wife, and the two will become one flesh." This is a profound mystery--but I am talking about Christ and the church. However, each one of you also must love his wife as he loves himself, and the wife must respect her husband. (Ephesians 5:21-32)

Here we learn that men are to love their wives as Christ loved the Church, that women are to reverence their husbands, and that in so doing, each Christian couple is to model, as the world observes their marriage, the wonderful hope of the Gospel.

We also learn that the Church is not yet *radiant* or *stain free*, but rather, *wrinkled* and *blemished*. Neither is she yet completely *Holy* or *blameless*. This is what she will be in Glory. Until then, like any husband or wife, the Church is tainted by sin. One day, she will be perfected. When it comes to expecting perfection we should have as realistic a view of the Church as we do of any other institution—after all, it's made up of human beings. The one *big* exception is that our expectations can be legitimately higher for an organization whose founder and head is Christ Himself; all that is good and right in the Church is of Christ. All that is flawed and sinful is of man. The real miracle is that He continues to entrust His Church to our stewardship at all. What a responsibility to dare take lightly! Remember the old saying: "If you find a perfect church, do not join it or it will no longer be perfect!"

There is a hedonistic dimension of church life that has always troubled me. I, along with other pastors, hear *ad nauseam* how the Church fails to meet someone's particular needs. Although it seems counterintuitive, the best way for your needs to be met in the Church is for you to meet the needs of others in sacrificial love and giving. Since you cannot out-give God, you *will* find true blessing in your church when you are selfless and other-oriented. But at the same time, step back and take a look at yourself in the mirror. We should Biblically expect Christ's Church to be a haven, a refuge and a healing balm for our hurts and failures. But, are you bringing the right "needs" with you when you join together with a group of other believers? If your expectations of the Church are other than what the Church was designed by Christ to satisfy, you are bound to be disappointed. Be certain to include in your "portfolio of personal needs" healthy portions of: 1) the need for fellowship with your God, 2) fellowship with His people, 3) instruction and exhortation from His Word, and 4) the re-equipping of yourself to go out and be salt and light to others who are perishing without the Gospel message!

The message to our kids is simple: parents, teach your children that the Church belongs to none other than Christ Himself. She is to be reverenced and loved and she deserves your loyalty. It is *His* Church, and He promised that the gates of hell will not stand against her (Matthew 16:18). Teach this to your children.

Reason #2: Wisdom has hewn out seven pillars upon which the Church is built.

...she has hewn out its seven pillars.
Proverbs 9:1b

In Scriptures, the number seven is the symbolic number of perfection or completeness. In the book of Revelation, for example, a reference that is made to the seven spirits of God doesn't mean that there are literally seven Holy Spirits; rather, it is simply stating that the number seven reflects the fullness and completeness of the Spirit of God (Revelation 1:4).

Proverbs 9:1 also tells us that she, Wisdom, has hewn out seven complete and "perfect pillars" that form the central structure of the house she has built. These pillars, or critical structural elements, are not man-made but rather God-made—complete, perfect and indestructible. The absence of or undermining of even one of these pillars causes the entire building to crumble. This is Satan's futile goal. Your children should learn that the Church they serve—the Church of Jesus Christ—stands firmly upon these seven pillars:

- The perfect and eternal covenant of Grace;
- The perfect incarnation of the perfect, infinite God-man—Jesus Christ;
- The perfect and sinless life Jesus lived;
- The perfect atonement and resurrection made for the sins of God's people;
- The perfect Holy Spirit that has been given to the Church;
- The perfect Holy Scriptures that guide us into all truth;
- The perfect and sovereign plan for our future and the consummation of the age.

The early Church fathers knew that the absolute uniqueness of Christ's Church stood or fell as these pillars stood or fell, and with Godly Wisdom instituted various creeds as solemn and historic "memory devices" to enable Christians throughout the ages to never lose sight of the seven perfect pillars.

Our children need to learn that God's eternal plan of redemption was not an afterthought. He did not create the world, watch as man fell into sin, and wring His hands in helpless despair. He did not cry out, "Oops. What am I going to do now?" There was no reactionary "Plan B." The perfect and eternal covenant of Grace was framed before creation. In eternity past, God the Father, God the Son and God the Holy Spirit purposed to save unto themselves an elect people. The eternal covenant of God's Grace through redemption is one of the perfect pillars of the Church.

It was this eternal and incredible covenant of Grace that, in the fullness of time, brought about the incarnation. God became a man, lived a perfect, sinless life, and willingly sacrificed His life to pay the price for the sins of His people. His life, and the singular purpose for which He came, reached its culmination when Jesus was crucified, died and was buried. But, having willingly laid down His life, He took it up again and death could not hold Him. Had He remained death's prisoner, there would be no salvation, and we would all be lost and without hope beyond the grave.

Paul ensured that there should be no confusion over the criticality of this "perfect pillar":

But if it is preached that Christ has been raised from the dead, how can some of you say that there is no resurrection of the dead? If there is no resurrection of the dead, then not even Christ has been raised. And if Christ has not been raised, our preaching is useless and so is your faith. More than that, we are then found to be false witnesses about God, for we have testified about God that he raised Christ from the dead. But he did not raise him if in fact the dead are not raised. For if the dead are not raised, then Christ has not been raised either. And if Christ has not been raised, your faith is futile; you are still in your sins. Then those also who have fallen asleep in Christ are lost. If only for this life we have hope in Christ, we are to be pitied more than all men. (1 Corinthians 15:12-19)

Did you catch that last phrase? If there were no resurrection, Christians would be a more pitiful lot than anyone else on earth for having been so shamelessly deceived. The incarnation, the life, death, burial and resurrection of Christ are among the perfect pillars upon which the Church is built and, not surprisingly, are the prime targets of all enemies who seek to discredit and destroy the Church.

Jesus made it very clear to His disciples that He would not always be with them physically. In fact, hours before His trial and death, Jesus prepared His disciples this way: *"But I tell you the truth: It is for your good that I am going away. Unless I go away, the Counselor will not come to you; but if I go, I will send him to you"* (John 16:7). What could possibly be better, from their point of view, than the physical presence of Jesus remaining with His disciples? But if Jesus had physically stayed with them after the resurrection, He would not have ascended into glory, back to His Father, and the plan of salvation would be incomplete without the glorification of the Son. In His high priestly prayer (the true Lord's Prayer, where we actually hear Jesus pray on his own behalf), Jesus concludes with these words: *"Father, I want those you have given me to be with me where I am, and to see my glory, the glory you have given me because you loved me before the creation of the world"* (John 17:24).

Although He would leave them physically, He would not leave them spiritually. He promised to return to them in the form of the Counselor. This is the promise of the Holy Spirit. That word, *Counselor*, is a special word; it is the picture of one who comes alongside another. He would not merely dwell among them, nor would He any longer occupy tents, temples and arks. This time, He promised to come back to fill and empower each of them individually.

When the day of Pentecost came, they were all together in one place. Suddenly a sound like the blowing of a violent wind came from heaven and filled the whole house where they were sitting. They saw what seemed to be tongues of fire that separated and came to rest on each of them. (Acts 2:1-3)

The Holy Spirit is the perfect Counselor, the perfect presence and power of Christ, who indwells each of us who have trusted in Him. The Holy Spirit guides us into all truth, but how does He do this?

"If anyone loves me, he will obey my teaching. My Father will love him, and we will come to him and make our home with him. He who does not love me will not obey my teaching. These words you hear are not my own; they belong to the Father who sent me. All this I have spoken while still with you. But the Counselor, the Holy Spirit, whom the Father will send in my name, will teach you all things and will remind you of everything I have said to you." (John 14:23-26)

The Holy Spirit teaches us and reminds us of all that Jesus Himself taught so that we might have continuous exposure to the Word of God in our lives and thereby be moved to obey Him. All that God wants to teach us is recorded in the Bible. It took nearly 70 years for the Canon of Scripture to be completed in the 66 books of the Bible we have today. The Holy Spirit made the Church the guardian of sacred Scripture. Christians believe, based on other proofs and the last sentence in the above passage, that God inspired various men to record His very words. The direct agent of these God-breathed words is the Holy Spirit. The Bible is God's revelation to man. It is primarily a faith commitment to trust your life and your eternity to the Bible and the Bible alone, but it is also reasonable that you do so—as God has said, *"Come, let us reason together"* (Isaiah 1:18). Be assured that your trust couldn't be better placed—absolutely no other collection of "religious" writings penned over such an expanse of time by so many diverse authors can hold a candle to the Bible. The consistency of its message, from Genesis to Revelation, its flawless prophetic and historical accuracy, and its survival through centuries of demonic assaults are what make this book unique.

Its timeless story of a Savior and a salvation plan that belie all other man-made paths to God, and the miraculously changed lives in those it has touched, leave no other explanation but that the God of the universe has condescended to speak to us through the pages of this book we call the Bible. It is perfect. It is complete. It is a pillar of the Church.

Teach your children that they can trust their lives and their eternity to the message of the Bible.

Reason #3: The Church has a message for the world and a method for distributing it.

She has prepared her meat and mixed her wine;
she has also set her table. She has sent out her maids,
and she calls from the highest point of the city.
Proverbs 9:2-3

Wisdom is on a mission. The preparations have already been made—the meal is ready, the table has been set, and trusted servants have been sent out with an important message. But just who are these "maids"? Who are the people whom God has entrusted to "call out" to millions of people around the world? The answer is His Church—the weak, imperfect myriad of servants who have been purchased by the blood of Christ.

Incredibly, God has not chosen any other way to herald His message of salvation but through His precious Church. As we have already learned from the parable found in Luke 14, we are to go into the city streets and the country lanes to call all men everywhere to repentance. In spite of our many faults and excuses, we can have boldness and confidence in knowing that Wisdom (i.e., Christ) has sent us out into the world to disseminate this marvelous and lifesaving message.

So, what is this message? We find it in the next three verses of Proverbs 9...

"Let all who are simple come in here!" she says to those who lack judgment. "Come, eat my food and drink the wine I have mixed. Leave your simple ways and you will live; walk in the way of understanding." (Proverbs 9:4-6)

In other words: *believe the Gospel*. Is there any message more exciting that we could ever possibly relay to a hurting and needy world?

With that said, there's one other thing to mention. The Church as we know it today has an abundance of programs—as a matter of fact, I believe that it's been programmed to death. Banners and billboards along the highways throughout this country advertise hundreds of church programs, promoting ministries for recovering addicts, help for the elderly and disabled, food for the hungry, and a host of others. Of course, there's nothing wrong with having programs. However, we err when we equate programs with the message of the Gospel. As part of God's Church, *we* are the instrument that takes His message out to a needy world, and we should remember that the effectiveness of the Church and its message is measured by our obedience to the Great Commission:

"Therefore go and make disciples of all nations, baptizing them in the name of the Father and of the Son and of the Holy Spirit, and teaching them to obey everything I have commanded you. And surely I am with you always, to the very end of the age." (Matthew 28:19-20)

Christ Himself, with a perfect Spirit of love and compassion, ministered to the practical needs of the hurting people around Him. But, He never did it with a motive of instituting bread lines and health clinics. He attracted people with His love and His miracles only to draw them to Himself and His message–the very purpose for which He came. The real compassion is in the offering of Himself as the bread of life in order to bring eternal healing to the sin-sick soul.

The fatal flaw in churches that have been spiritually dying over recent generations is their well-intentioned, but misinformed, efforts to emphasize only the "social gospel" of meeting the physical and emotional needs of their communities at the expense of abandoning the Gospel message for which Christ gave His life. The natural outcome of "losing the message" is a growing tolerance for all of the false, "equally valid" ways of "finding God" that we see in the cults that are gaining so many followers today. These dying Christian churches have disobeyed the Great Commission and have abandoned their guard duty—and lost souls are paying the price.

We must teach our children how to take that message into their mission fields, their personal circles of influence—their homes, jobs, friendships and family. They must learn both the method *and* the message of the Church. They are the method; salvation through Christ and Christ alone is the message. They should never grow up to fall in love with "programs," believing that the Church's message is only about singing in the choir, or attending youth groups, Bible studies or Sunday school. If they fail to understand and embrace the methodology that God has chosen in order to spread His message, our children will never have an evangelistic fervor for the lost people of the world. Given that all church "programs" should be, above all, Christ-centered and message-centered, their only Biblical purpose for existence is to "equip the saints" (that's *you*, believer!) to take the light and hope of the salvation message, with compassion, into a lost, dark world.

Like every other concept I've tried to convey in this book, the mission and message of the Church is a principle that forces us to examine our own hearts before we are able to communicate its truth to our children. Do *we*, as Christian parents, possess our own evangelistic fervor for the lost? Are we convinced that the Church is not just four walls, pews and pulpits, but rather, a spiritual kingdom we must learn to love as Howard and Barbara Weldin loved it? Let us strive to raise a generation of children who look beyond the flaws, the weaknesses, and the inconsistencies, in order to love—truly *love*—God's Church.

Teaching Moments

• The best way to teach is to live what you believe. God's view of the Church, as outlined in this chapter, is comprised of large truths that can only be passed on to our children if we embrace them, not just with our minds and our hearts, but in outward practice. Spend time studying the Scriptures and principles in this chapter and note how these principles will inform you as you attempt to resolve the next conflict you face in your local church.

• Read through with your children the Apostle's Creed and the Nicene Creed and start helping them to commit it to memory.

• Commit to treating your local church family in a way that reflects Christ, even when you disagree with them. Teach your children how to resolve conflict by the way you react when you do not like the worship music, the length of the pastor's sermon or his message, the direction of the church, or the most recent congregational vote.

• Resolve never to speak with anger or hatred toward your local church in front of your children.

• When you pray with your children, pray fervently for your church family, pastors and leadership team. Write out the names of your pastor, leaders, missionaries, ministry leaders, etc. on 3 x 5 cards. Give each child the opportunity to pick a card every day and to pray for that person or ministry outreach. For very young children, talk to them about their favorite program at church (Sunday school, family night, basketball league, etc.) and explain how their leader or coach needs them to pray with thanksgiving for them, for their families, etc. This type of praying will personalize and connect your child more deliberately to the bigger picture of the church family.

• Place all your Christmas cards in a basket. Throughout the year, at breakfast or dinner, ask one of your children to choose a card and then pray for that family. This practice will not only impact the families for whom you are praying but will teach your children the power and importance of their responsibility to help carry the burdens of their covenant family—their church.

• Teach your children responsibility for taking care of their local church building. Many years ago we observed a couple in our church taking their young children up and down the rows of pews after services, picking up extra bulletins, tissues, etc., and placing hymnals back into the racks. They started this practice when their children were toddlers. Now their grown up children are mission-minded, always serving others and sold-out to loving their local churches. Young children love doing grown-up deeds that they observe their parents doing with joy.

---

[1] "Christmas at the Last House Standing," http://www.cnn.com/2008/US/12/22/last.house.irpt/index.html

CHAPTER TEN
Pearls, Pigs, Scorners and Mockers

Teach Your Children This Story

MANY YEARS AGO, a young man named Roy Riegels played football for the University of California at Berkeley. He only played for two years, but his "wrong way" run during a very important game would become the most famous blunder in college football history!

It was January 1, 1929, and Roy's team, the Golden Bears, was facing the Georgia Tech Yellow Jackets in the Rose Bowl game in Pasadena, California. About halfway through the second quarter, Roy managed to pick up the ball after a fumble by the Yellow Jackets. As he started toward the opposing team's end zone, he was suddenly shoved in the direction of a Yellow Jackets tackler. In his efforts to get away from him, Roy somehow veered too far off course and lost his bearings. Although he was just 30 yards away from the Yellow Jackets' goal line and seconds from scoring a touchdown for his team, Roy spun around and took off, running full steam ahead with aggressive determination—in the *wrong* direction!

The Golden Bears quarterback, Benny Lom, began chasing Roy as he sprinted toward his own end zone, screaming all the while for him to stop. It wasn't until Roy had run over 65 yards that Benny finally caught up to him. But, even though he managed to turn him around at the 3-yard line, Roy was instantly tackled by a swarm of Georgia Tech players.

Roy retreated to the locker room at halftime where he draped a blanket around his shoulders, buried his face in his hands and cried. When halftime was over, Roy was the only player who didn't head back out to the field. "Coach, I can't do it," he cried. "I've ruined you. I've ruined my school. I've ruined myself. I couldn't face the crowd in that stadium to save my life."

"Roy, get up and go back," the coach encouraged him. "The game is only half over."

Roy Riegels did return to the football field and played well for the rest of the game. The Golden Bears, unfortunately, still lost by a score of 8-7.

Following the game, the coach charitably defended Roy's blunder as "an accident that might have happened to anyone." And despite the national fame that earned him the nickname "Wrong Way" Riegels, the young man graduated from college and went on to live a very successful life.

Parenting Principle: You must teach your children how to deal with scorn.

Whoever corrects a mocker invites insult;
whoever rebukes a wicked man incurs abuse.
Do not rebuke a mocker or he will hate you;
rebuke a wise man and he will love you.
Proverbs 9:7-8

The woman Folly is loud; she is undisciplined
and without knowledge. She sits at the door of her house,
on a seat at the highest point of the city, calling out to
those who pass by, who go straight on their way.
"Let all who are simple come in here!" she says to those
who lack judgment. "Stolen water is sweet; food eaten in

*secret is delicious!" But little do they know that the dead
are there, that her guests are in the depths of the grave.*
Proverbs 9:13-18

Several months ago, I had lunch with a missionary. Dan was a church-sponsored missionary whom I hadn't seen for many years, in part because he had spent the past two decades sharing the Good News of Christ on the mission field in Japan. Accompanied by a Japanese pastor, along with that pastor's family, Dan returned to the United States for a visit with some key pastors to explore and clarify their overall vision for the Japanese churches.

From the time the old station wagon weighed down with people drove into our church parking lot, the Japanese pastor and his family were overwhelmingly amazed—not just at the size of the church property (something that would be an impossible dream for a Christian church in Japan!), but also at the variety of ministries God enabled us to offer to our large congregation. Neither the pastor nor his wife spoke English, but as their jaws dropped at the sights all around them, one word they uttered was very clear: *"Wow!"* How was it possible that one church could have so much?

Lunch was at a small Italian restaurant where Dan wasted no time in opening a witnessing opportunity with the waitress who approached our table. When he learned that the woman was a Christian, he asked if she would remember to pray for his church in Japan. The waitress suggested that we all pray together—right then and there. Then, the pastor's wife led our group in prayer (in Japanese) for the waitress as Dan interpreted.

The Japanese pastor was moved to tears by what he had just seen and heard. In all of his 19 years of ministry in Japan, he never, *ever* met another Christian in a public setting, let alone actually prayed with one in public. As I continued talking (via Dan's interpretation) with my new Japanese brother in Christ, I learned that he had recently given up a good pastoral position in order to begin a fresh ministry of church-planting, literally starting his career all over again, despite the fact that his congregation loved him and begged him not to go. Without a doubt, I knew that I was in the presence of a man who truly *loved* God's Church, overcame disillusionment and remained driven by his burden for lost souls.

As we discussed the Japanese culture, he clearly demonstrated his grasp of how his people think and what elements are shaping their worldview. His daunting task was to teach his church how to think strategically, how to reason along Biblical lines, and how to deploy the Gospel in a setting where a Christian is not to be acknowledged in public. To many of us Americans, this unfamiliar dimension of Christian ministry would seem to be very challenging, if not impossible, to say the least! We all discussed at length the state of the American church. We agreed that, although the Church here appeared, on the surface, to be better off and enjoyed more liberties than the Church in Japan, things were not what they seemed to be. We talked together of the divisions in our culture—racial, political, social, philosophical and economic—that have nearly torn this country apart. Cracks in our "shining mansion on a hill" have widened, with a full scale collapse from within seeming imminent.

Sadly, these divisions, along with other causes, have resulted in the evangelical Church slowly but surely losing her spiritual uniqueness and public credibility. Instead of training young men and women to engage their cultures, we teach them how to major on minors and to play Trivial Pursuit, church style.

Divisions in the Church derail effective discipleship, resulting in an entirely new generation that does not know how to think critically or Biblically, and crumbles when faced with intellectual argument. This new generation has been raised on a steady diet of spiritual mediocrity, trivial pursuits, flawed worship and theological compromise. Now we have a new kind of Church member—one who *likes* the Church, provided his or her personal needs are met, but does not truly *love* or *serve* the Church for the long haul. The hard work of learning how to think Biblically is left to others, leaving the resultant, weak-minded Christian a sitting duck for the fiery darts of the Wicked One.

Maybe it's high time for American Christians who harbor a commitment-optional, country-club mentality toward church membership to take a lesson from our Christian brothers and sisters in Japan and other parts of the world. Where identification with Christ carries a heavy personal price tag, and finding a Bible-centered church in which to worship isn't so easy, people tend to not take their faith so lightly.

Children must learn that the enemies of the Gospel are real.

Whoever corrects a mocker invites insult; whoever rebukes a wicked man incurs abuse. Do not rebuke a mocker or he will hate you; rebuke a wise man and he will love you. (Proverbs 9:7-8)

There are two types of mockers, the *ignorant mocker* and the *willful mocker*, and both are enemies of the Gospel. We find an example of the *ignorant mocker* in the book of 1 Timothy, where the Apostle Paul describes what he was like before he became a Christian...

"Even though I was once a blasphemer and a persecutor and a violent man, I was shown mercy because I acted in ignorance and unbelief." (1 Timothy 1:13)

In the book of Acts, we read about the second type of scorner, the *willful mocker*...
When the Jews saw the crowds, they were filled with jealousy and talked abusively against what Paul was saying.

Then Paul and Barnabas answered them boldly: "We had to speak the word of God to you first. Since you reject it and do not consider yourselves worthy of eternal life, we now turn to the Gentiles..." But the Jews incited the God-fearing women of high standing and the leading men of the city. They stirred up persecution against Paul and Barnabas, and expelled them from their region. (Acts 13:45-46, 50)

Both types are linked to rebellion against God—Paul, a violent blasphemer who once persecuted the Church out of ignorance and unbelief, versus the well-informed, yet stubborn Jews, who intentionally rejected the Word of God and abused the messengers who came to deliver it.

Although our children will undoubtedly be exposed to mockers, the Gospel is too Holy to be offered as a target for those whose only purpose is to mock God's Word—as Jesus Himself warned in the book of Matthew...

"Do not give dogs what is sacred; do not throw your pearls to pigs. If you do, they may trample them under their feet, and then turn and tear you to pieces." (Matthew 7:6)

This warning is rooted in Proverbs 9:7-8. To correct a mocker, or as Jesus put it, to cast pearl before pigs, is to invite harm not only to the pearl (the Gospel) but also to the one who delivers the Gospel. While some will be open to the Gospel and may even come to embrace its lifesaving message, there are many who will not be interested, and it is a small leap from disinterest to outright mockery against God and His Word. It is prudent to be able to spot the difference between the ignorant mocker and the willful mocker. It is when faced with the willful mocker (the King James Version uses the word *scorner*) that we must teach our children to avoid the trap of falling into argumentativeness and vitriol. As witnesses for Christ, the Church is to be about Holy business and not about staining her reputation by rolling in the mud with mockers.

When I became a Christian at the age of nineteen, my first exposure to the ignorant mocker came from members of my own family, many of whom have since come to know Christ. They simply did not understand what had happened to me, and I did not communicate the Gospel with love. It was only after I recognized my error and sought forgiveness that I discovered a brand new open door to my family. They were mockers at first, but only out of ignorance. Because God helped me distinguish between ignorant and willful mockery, sincere hearts were opened, and as a result, I will be enjoying a much larger reunion with loved ones in Glory when I arrive.

However, my first exposure to the willful mocker came when I attended the Billy Graham School of Evangelism at Madison Square Garden in New York City. After one of the late night meetings, a man climbed a soap box on a street corner next to the Garden and began to lace Billy Graham and the message of the Gospel with nasty epithets. My first reaction was to stand up to his insults and defend Mr. Graham and the Gospel. So, that is what I did—until I felt someone grab my arm and pull me backwards. He was one of the leaders in the school. I will never forget what he told me: "Sir, this is not how God wants us to spread the Gospel. Do not allow this man to engage you in this way. It degrades the Gospel. He is a mocker and God does not want us to give credence to mockers." This encounter had all of the makings of an all-out vitriolic exchange that would have effectually turned a debate into a verbal brawl.

Cultivating the fear of God in ourselves and others is sacred business because our God is Holy. Living out the Gospel in a world filled with mockers is not a game or an intellectual competition. This is why the Gospel must not be sacrificed on the altar of casualness. We must not "play church" as two little toddlers might "play house." The Church is to guard and preserve the purity of the pearl that is the Gospel. Our children will encounter many mockers in life and some will be ignorant, while others will be willful. We must teach them how to identify the difference and respond accordingly.

Mockers are the very same people who mark the weak and the unwise and target them for attack. We need not go any further to demonstrate this than the typical, secular, university professor. It is a story repeated over and over again, sadly, with increasing frequency. The scenario goes something like this–a young believer leaves his or her high school and church community and heads off to the university campus, holding strong to what they had been taught since childhood. They take a class in history or literature or philosophy where some self-proclaimed intellectual challenges their faith with the tough questions their moms, dads, and church teachers never prepared them to answer. They sit there dumbfounded and defeated. Their faith has been mocked in front of dozens of onlookers by the *willful mocker* and they are impotent to deal with it.

There is a legitimate place for intellectual apologetics (defense of the faith) and polemics (the offensive confrontation of falsehood and misrepresentation) when opportunities arise, especially in the classroom. But when common civility and the sincere exchange of viewpoints cross over into ridicule, close-mindedness and mockery, you are now casting pearls to an obviously unreceptive person and you need not waste yours or God's time. Certainly, the college campus—in contrast to a street corner melee—is an incubator for such spiritual exercises. We must teach our children not only the facts of the Gospel, but how to think and express themselves. They make some meager effort at arguing with the professor, or any mocker, only to be mocked even more. The result is that the faith of the ill-prepared child is shattered and the Gospel is ridiculed– reemphasizing the accuracy of Proverbs 9:7, *Whoever corrects a mocker invites insult; whoever rebukes a wicked man incurs abuse.*

Stunned in the face of such arrogant unbelief, the young man or woman becomes disoriented and begins to head the wrong way with their life, without even fully understanding what has taken place. Like "Wrong Way" Riegels, they sprint toward the opponent's end zone while the *willful mocker* cheers them on and their own teammates (the core values you taught them) are feverishly trying to redirect them before it's too late. All that you have taught your child is suddenly jeopardized by the *willful mocker* with the outcome being your son's or daughter's moral and spiritual failure. We all too often hear an adult's testimony that goes something like this: "When I was a child, I was raised in the church. I came to know the Lord at a very young age. But when I went to college, I drifted away from Him and lived a self-indulgent life of drinking, drugs and sex. Then, after college, I rededicated my life to the Lord."

What causes this spiritual hiatus? Among other things, we are all vulnerable to a spiritual disease that makes us "brittle," and shatters our Christian resolve at merely the slightest hint of personal attack or cynicism. The chief symptom of this disease is frailty of mind or the inability to think clearly. The challenge for us as parents is to teach our children early how to think analytically, to reason, to defend what they believe, to spot the counterfeit, and to value the pearl of the Gospel. When they are young they need to be prepared to address the questions the unbelieving world will ask, and to overcome, where possible, the sincere inquirer's objections and difficulties with the Gospel. There are many good books, tapes, and videos designed to do this. However, whatever Scripturally-solid resources you use, nothing is more critical to teaching your children how and when to defend their beliefs than grounding them in the truth of the Gospel before they become teenagers (see **Teaching Moments** at the end of this chapter).

They must always strive to become risk-taking disciples in a world of great challenges and surprises. They will occasionally fail and you must be there to make sure that they "fail forward." Just like the coach who encouraged "Wrong Way" Riegels back onto the football field, we must lift their wounded souls, dust off their embarrassment, and send them right back into the game armed with our support and a fresh quiver full of arrows to answer the faith-shattering and faith-defiant, fiery darts of the mockers.

Jesus often sparred with extremely willful mockers such as the Scribes and Pharisees. Old Testament saints and prophets were verbal and physical warriors in the defense of God's Word and God's honor—in the faces of all mockers! A verbal response should, of course, be given graciously and respectfully, knowing when to cut it off. But it should still always be given to everyone and every opportunity should be taken!

Be wise in the way you act toward outsiders; make the most of every opportunity. Let your conversation be always full of grace, seasoned with salt, so that you may know how to answer everyone. (Colossians 4:5-6)

The student confronted by the professor didn't have to get into a knock-down, drag-out, extended debate for which she was not equipped, but *every* believer is equipped—and commanded—to give a simple, gentle answer for the hope that is in them with a brief testimony, and let God be responsible for ensuring that His Word will not return empty.

"As the rain and the snow come down from heaven, and do not return to it without watering the earth and making it bud and flourish, so that it yields seed for the sower and bread for the eater, so is my Word that goes out from my mouth: It will not return to me empty, but will accomplish what I desire and achieve the purpose for which I sent it." (Isaiah 55:10-11)

Children must learn that the enemies of the Gospel are formidable.

Let's face it: Satan is no less earnest in seeking to destroy the lives of God's people than Jesus is to save them. He's a formidable foe. Let's take a look at what the Proverbs have to say about this great enemy of God's Church...

The woman Folly is loud; she is undisciplined and without knowledge. (Proverbs 9:13)

The definition of the word *loud* in this passage is rather interesting. Rarely used in the Scriptures, it's a word that describes the arousing of the senses in order to get the passions of lust and rebellion spinning out of control. This word is an earmark of all sin—clamorous, turbulent and animated by passion. It's a word that describes one continuous, loud, monotonous noise with the specific purpose of incitement and provocation.

Remarkably, yet prophetically, it seems as if the loudest voices in our society today are the ones screaming for more rights to sin—such as the right to kill an unborn child, to marry a gay partner or to propagate pornography and vulgarity. The loudest voices are rarely clamoring for holiness and Godliness. Yet, amid this clamor of unbelief, God speaks through the still, small voice of the Spirit, available to all who love and trust Him and who are willing to practice the disciplines of Grace—that is, the study of the Word, fervent and effectual prayer, and worship that is focused and intertwined with the expectation that, as we engage God, He engages us and will change us to be effective witnesses for Him.

But there is much more to be said in the characterization of this foe we face:
She sits at the door of her house, on a seat at the highest point of the city, calling out to those who pass by, who go straight on their way. "Let all who are simple come in

here!" she says to those who lack judgment. (Proverbs 9:14-16)

*On a seat at the highest point of the city...*Our foe is not only loud but shameless. Do you recall a time when certain sins were considered shameful? We now pride ourselves in our license, liberality and tolerance. All the while, the enemy calls out to those who lack judgment from his perch on high.

The Prince of Darkness lusts for the mind of your child. And since, by definition, lust can never be satisfied, and since our enemy cannot have those of us, as parents, who have already trusted Christ, he will surely make a strong play for our children. Be always aware that Satan will not approach your child with offers and propositions that are frightening and distasteful:

"Stolen water is sweet; food eaten in secret is delicious!" (Proverbs 9:17)

The foe deceives us by presenting sin as pleasurable and inconsequential. And let's face it—sin *is* pleasurable! Yet, illicit pleasures have horizontal and vertical consequences: *But little do they* (sinners) *know that the dead are there, that her guests are in the depths of the grave* (Proverbs 9:18). As far back as the Garden, Adam and Eve tragically learned that... *The soul that sins is the one who will die* (Ezekiel 18:20). God has never rescinded that fearful promise.

When all is said and done, we can always be sure of one thing: the enemy's end *will* be death—for all eternity. But in the meantime, we can also be certain that Satan wants our children as his guests in the depths of the grave, and he'll do whatever is necessary to take them there. The battle for the soul of your child must never be underestimated. And this side of Glory we will never be free and clear of his devices.

Children are easily disillusioned. Their emotions drive them to tears one minute and to laughter the next. When they become teenagers, their sensitivities become more intense. Whether in college, or even in the workplace, they will need to have their passions and their emotions under control or that bitter taste of spiritual warfare will undo what you have taken years to accomplish in them. This is why, early in the process, God exhorts parents and children as follows:

Children, obey your parents in the Lord, for this is right. "Honor your father and mother"—which is the first commandment with a promise—"that it may go well with you and that you may enjoy long life on the earth." Fathers, do not exasperate your children; instead, bring them up in the training and instruction of the Lord. (Ephesians 6:1-4)

It all boils down to...*teaching them young!*

Teaching Moments

• It is important that your children learn how to share the Gospel. Not only will they be obeying the Great Commission, but they will also be applying the practical aspects of the Gospel by teaching to others what they are learning from you. I encourage every believer to identify the "Ten Most Wanted" in their circles of influence. All of us live in a circle of family, friends, neighbors, classmates, co-workers, and even enemies. In that circle of influence, there are some who are more open to the Gospel than others. They could even be called the *ignorant mockers*, but they are worth the investment of time and energy. Since we are not to argue but rather to share the Gospel, begin by helping your children share their faith patiently and graciously. With your children, identify ten people in their network of relationships who are most likely to respond. It would be very effective and a good confidence-builder if you would "role-play" the sharing of the Gospel with your saved child. You pretend to be a "polite" unbeliever, and your child can "safely" share her faith within her age-appropriate level of understanding.

• Begin early to teach them how to handle the most common objections to the Gospel. There are a myriad of books on this topic. Google "apologetics for children" to begin your search. Among some more advanced resources, better suited to helping parents, and adults in general, defend what and why they believe, are books such as Josh McDowell's *Evidence That Demands a Verdict*; Frank Morrison's *Who Moved the Stone?*; D. James Kennedy's *Why I Believe*; Walter R. Martin's *The Kingdom of the Cults*, and a host of other age-appropriate resources.

• Teach your children to memorize the shorter catechism. Visit us at www.markinc.org to order your copy.

CONCLUSION
Finishing Well

Teach Your Children This Story

Down for the Count–Dave Tiberi

ON FEBRUARY 8, 1992, I sat glued to my television set as a local boxer, a young Christian man who also happened to be a good friend of mine, Dave Tiberi, entered the ring to contend for the IBF Middleweight Championship of the World. He was the decided underdog, up against the reigning champion, James Toney. In fact, the gambling connections would not even take bets on the fight since it was generally felt that Tiberi had no chance of winning. Toney was described by Dan Dierdorf, the ABC ring announcer, as "a man who says he was born angry" whereas Tiberi was half-mockingly characterized as "a man of God."

I couldn't help wincing as Dave took a sharp and brutal right hook square on his forehead in the first round. Dave later told me he had never been hit so hard in his life and thought he was a goner. That, in fact, is just what Toney had promised, prior to the fight, to do to Dave: "I want to kill him." It may have been only pre-fight hype, but, nonetheless, that was one incredibly powerful punch.

I started yelling, "Go down, Dave! Don't be a hero. Go down! You are going to get killed!"

Dave, however, did not go down. Instead, he kept fighting and, as the fight progressed, he actually seemed to gain strength. He will tell you today that this strength came from the Lord Jesus. Dave desired nothing in those crucial, pain-filled, exhausting moments, other than to do his best. Of course, he wanted to win the title, but there was more at stake here for Dave. He wanted very much to bring glory to God in this bout. To be the middleweight champion of the world would give him name recognition and significant opportunities to honor God. Dave was certain, as he once told me, that, "boxing is my angle to witness to people."

With each round, it became more and more obvious to everyone, including the ringside announcers, that Dave had not only survived that early shot to the head, but—to everyone's surprise—was actually out-boxing his opponent and winning the fight. Though Sharon had no interest in watching two men "beat each other's brains out," she was drawn into the room by my excitement and uncontrolled shouting. She cautiously joined me, "just for a moment," to watch the action. By the eighth round, we were both thoroughly engrossed, both yelling and jumping and cheering for Dave. By the twelfth round, I was practically screaming at the television, "Stay away from Toney, Dave! You won! You won!"

When, at last, the final bell sounded, I was ecstatic. "You did it, Dave! You did it! You won!" The announcers, the news reporters, and most sports fans around the world saw what we just saw and were convinced that "underdog" Dave was clearly the victor.

Two of the three judges who scored the fight, however, somehow saw it all quite differently and they awarded the match to James Toney. We, and many others along with us, were absolutely astounded by that decision. Our friend Dave was devastated.

Sharon and I had just witnessed one of the greatest injustices in boxing history. The awarding of the decision to James Toney eventually led Senator William Roth of Delaware to ask for a Senate investigation into the sport of boxing. This unjust decision confronted Dave head-on with an extraordinarily difficult test of his faith. At that moment, Dave did not have "Genesis 50:20 vision," the ability to appreciate and accept all that happens—even our greatest disappointments and personal crises—as part of God's good and perfect will for us. The verse reads, *"you intended to harm me, but God intended it for good."* Blindsided by the judges' decision, Dave was not prepared for what this severe and painful disappointment would bring him. After the fight, this frustrated and confused young boxer could only tell interviewers that he had been "deprived." The ringside announcer, less restrained, called it "a disgusting decision."

God, however, was able to take that act of injustice and use it for good in Dave's life. Defeat forced Dave to carefully consider how he might be able to glorify God even in the midst of his disappointment. As Dave later told me, "Each time God helped me to obey Him by responding honestly, but without malice, to my circumstances, I experienced a little bit more of His peace. I began to realize that He had intentionally arranged this entire situation for His own eternal reason."

Thus, the loss of that fight, tactically speaking, gave Dave greater name recognition and opened up more ministry opportunities than a win could possibly have done. This Godly man is now enjoying an ever-widening circle of influence among growing television audiences and inner-city young people. He deliberately located the Dave Tiberi Youth Center right in the middle of the most active illegal drug neighborhoods in Wilmington, Delaware, where no other youth ministries existed. Dave's Godly response to his unfair treatment has earned him the right to share the hope of Christ with teens who have been similarly betrayed by people and systems that were supposed to uphold justice and protect them. God is transforming a bitterly unjust defeat into eternal victories. He has used this experience not only to deepen Dave's peace in his own journey but also to deepen and strengthen the faith of many others.[1]

Parenting Principle: Teach your children how to deal with disillusionment and finish well.

The fear of the Lord is the beginning of wisdom, and knowledge of the Holy One is understanding. For through me your days will be many, and years will be added to your life. If you are wise, your wisdom will reward you; if you are a mocker, you alone will suffer.
Proverbs 9:10-12

And so, we come full circle. In the first chapter, we focused on Proverbs 1:7: *The fear of the Lord is the beginning of knowledge, but fools despise wisdom and discipline.* It is appropriate that we end this book with Solomon's repetitive call to understand that all knowledge and Wisdom starts with the fear of the Lord.

By now you realize that I avoid simplistic "parenting recipes"; that is, I don't believe there are ten easy steps to raising a successful, happy child. Children are God's unique creation and come in a rainbow of "varieties." They cannot be categorized with a one-size-fits-all mentality. Parenting is hard work, even when it is laced with God's Grace. We ought to fill our children's minds with all the right knowledge, but each child must eventually choose to make the faith they have been taught and witnessed their own.

Instead of trying to protect our children from all pain, we must see childhood crises as opportunities to equip them to confront adult-sized disillusionment, disappointments and failures with eternity in view. When pain, mistakes and failure impact our children, we, as parents, need to understand that normal, everyday life presents them with the opportunity to either view their circumstances through the "fear-of-God-grid," or, in essence, abandon the "faith of their fathers" and turn to the "fear-of-man-grid."

A young teacher once shared this story. "I love teaching, but mediating the petty fighting that accompanies playground activities wore me down. 'It's not fair!' is the constant mantra of the young children in their bickering, and my usual patience in dealing with this repetitious cry all period long finally drove me to the wall. As is typical with most childish fights, I had no idea who was telling the truth, so I made a desperate decision to enforce the taking of turns on the swings. The second-grade complainant whined, 'But that's not fair!' I admit it—I lost my cool and yelled at the stunned students, 'Well guess what? Life isn't fair so get used to it!' Then I stomped away. I guess my outburst got their attention because there were no more fights on the playground that day."

I have to wonder if our friend's politically incorrect response seared the minds of a few of those children in a way that might just protect them from unrealistic expectations in their own life journeys. Life isn't fair from our perspective, but it is fair from God's. He holds the puzzle parts and He's the one weaving the tapestry. We can and must trust Him to work all things together for our good, in the unspeakably beautiful final design He has in mind for each of us.

Dave Tiberi's experience in the boxing ring is a startling reminder that what appears to be injustice to us is, in fact, exactly what God planned for us in His eternal purpose. Dave had to make a choice to face disillusionment while trusting God's truth, or give in to his natural emotions. This was not an easy struggle for him. He was robbed of the prize that was rightfully his. To finish well though, Dave had to exchange bitterness and anger for trust in the sovereignty of God and surrender to His eternal purposes. He had to go back to his foundational worldview that *the fear of God is the beginning of knowledge* (Proverbs 1:7) and the promise that, *if you are wise, your wisdom will reward you; if you are a mocker, you alone will suffer* (Proverbs 9:12). If Dave had reacted as a mocker and refused the pathway of God's Wisdom, his life would have been a mockery of his faith and he would have missed the peace and Grace that God had planned for him in the middle of an unfair and unjust life circumstance.

Whatever happens in our lives, if we are parents, we must realize that our responses to life's daily close encounters will influence our children in their own life journeys. In other words, it's not about us, but about reflecting redemption for our children to observe, and about teaching them by example how to walk by faith.

Disillusionment Because of Sincere Intentions

Wise parents must determine when their children's mistakes are rooted in deliberate disobedience, childish irresponsibility, or a wrong interpretation of instructions or circumstances. In the story at the beginning of Chapter 10, "Wrong Way" Riegels was sincere in running the wrong way. But he was sincerely wrong. His coach exhorted him the same way Jesus exhorted Saul, soon to be called Paul.

In Acts 9:1-6, Paul is described as *still breathing out murderous threats against the Lord's disciples. He went to the high priest and asked him for letters to the synagogues in Damascus, so that if he found any there who belonged to The Way, whether men or women, he might take them as prisoners to Jerusalem.* Saul's campaign to root out Christians resulted in imprisonment and martyrdom for many believers. He was convinced that he was God's man, prosecuting blasphemers and protecting God's reputation. But Saul was sincerely wrong. On his way to wreak havoc on unsuspecting men and women, a bright light from heaven flashes all around him and he falls to the ground. He hears a voice saying, *"Saul, Saul, why do you persecute me?"* (Acts 9:4) Now, don't miss the high emotion of this moment. Saul is terrified and pleads, *"Who are you, Lord?"* *"I am Jesus, whom you are persecuting,"* a voice replies. *"Now GET UP and go into the city, and you will be told what you must do"* (Acts 9:5-7) (emphasis added). Saul quickly and fearfully obeys, but is now blind and doesn't eat or drink anything for three days.

There is so much we can learn from this brief roadside encounter, but I want us to focus on the response of Jesus to Saul's misplaced but sincere intentions. We must imprint this same exhortation on the minds of our children so that when they experience disillusionment, whether it is a result of their own mistakes or the unfairness of life, they hear their parents' voices calling: "Get up."

How do you respond when you realize your actions have caused great pain to another? Rationalization? Explanations? Deep regret and guilt? Jesus gave Saul no time to lick his wounds. Instead, He commanded, "Get up and go!"

We must teach our children likewise. When their own mistakes create havoc in their lives or the lives of others, we must not allow them to wallow in self-pity. Saul recognized his terrible mistake and immediately followed Jesus' instructions. That obedience led him to forgiveness, restoration and a very productive future relationship with his Savior.

Disillusionment Because of Injustice

The fear of the Lord teaches a man wisdom,
and humility comes before honor.
Proverbs 15:33

Our son, Chuck, attended the University of Delaware on a full scholarship in Piano Performance. He then earned his Master's Degree in Piano Performance on a full scholarship to Temple University. But Chuck experienced grave disappointment in his quest to achieve these hard-earned awards. When he was in high school, he auditioned to compete in the regional Fine Arts Festival. Two other students auditioned along with Chuck for the two available spots. Chuck memorized an entire Beethoven sonata and played it well for the audition. One of the other students played the exact same piece that Chuck had played, except that he used written sheet music that he had not completely learned. Since these other students were well connected in the school, they were given the two spots and Chuck was left out. Our son took his case to the principal of the school, who was also his basketball coach. The principal told Chuck to "get over it" and that he needed to choose between piano and basketball.

A few years later in college, Chuck auditioned in a competition to play with a symphony orchestra. He learned the very difficult Rachmaninoff Second Piano Concerto, and it was apparent in all the auditions that he would win. His tryout was flawless and everyone agreed that no one else in the competition came close to his level of performance. His teacher believed it was a "slam dunk," that Chuck had won the competition and would be performing with the orchestra later that spring. We all were shocked to learn that another musician was given this coveted honor. Chuck was devastated and concluded that he must not have the gifts or talent that we encouraged him to believe he had. He knew he could not have competed more perfectly; every note was exact. Everyone agreed that the other musician was nowhere near the artist that Chuck was. Even that artist admitted the same to Chuck. How could this have happened?

His teacher learned that the competition winner was already a member of the orchestra and that this was his last opportunity to participate in one of their important performances. So the judges decided that, since Chuck could compete again the next year, the other young man should be given the award as a thank-you gift for his previous work with the orchestra.

Unfair? Disillusioned with the process? Broken trust? You bet. We had to talk Chuck through the process of how *a simple man believes anything, but a prudent man gives thought to his steps* (Proverbs 14:15). If he was a "simple man" he would believe the mocking in his soul—that he wasn't good enough, or that life isn't fair, so what's the point of trying. He could conclude that all honest effort was futile and that he would not subject himself to this type of heartbreaking stress again. Or he could be a prudent man and accept that life isn't fair and that God's purposes in giving the award to another student were part of a bigger plan. For Chuck to win the scholarships that underwrote his education he had to compete with other musicians. This setback could have derailed his continuing education. Chuck had to "get up and go," and use this as an opportunity to prepare for the tough competitions ahead. Instead of giving up, Chuck competed again the next year and won. The night of his performance, the auditorium was packed with more people than the event had ever attracted before. In fact, many people could not even get tickets.

A few years later, Chuck was asked to participate in a Master's class at Temple University. The professor conducting the class was a well-known pianist with a stellar reputation in his field. We watched during performance evaluations as this professor tore apart the first student's piece. We shuddered to think of how Chuck would react if he was subjected to the same treatment. Would he be able to take the criticism? But instead of criticism, the professor praised Chuck's technique and his skillful handling of the piece. After the class, he asked Chuck to be his student and offered him a full scholarship to Temple University.

From the time he was a child, we taught Chuck that disappointment was not the end of the road but an opportunity to "get up and go," to face the challenge of disillusionment armed with confidence that God's plan for His life could never be thwarted.

Teach your children to handle disappointment through the grid of God's Wisdom. Remind them that *in his heart a man plans his course* (and we should make plans), *but the Lord determines his steps* (Proverbs 16:9).

Disillusionment Because of Disappointment with God

He who fears the Lord, has a secure fortress,
and for his children it will be a refuge.
The fear of the Lord is a fountain of life,
turning a man from the snares of death.
Proverbs 14:26-27

Our greatest challenge to reflect our trust in God's sovereign love started on the night of July 6, 1993.

Our son, Mark, and his friend, Kelly, spent the evening in our home. Around 10:30 p.m., Mark left to take Kelly home. At about 11:00 p.m., we started getting phone calls from Kelly's frantic parents as they were wondering where she was. Unbeknownst to us, Kelly had a strict 11:00 p.m. curfew and had never missed it. By 11:30, Kelly's dad was out looking for Mark and Kelly. And at 11:45, we received the phone call that every parent dreads. I heard Sharon gasp when she was told, "This is the hospital. Your son has been in an accident. You need to come right away."

I drove over 100 mph, desperate to find out if Mark was still alive. We passed the horrific accident scene and I grabbed Sharon's hand. "This isn't good," I said in an attempt to prepare her for what I now knew in my heart we were about to face.

After what seemed like an eternity, we finally arrived at the hospital. I watched as Sharon ran to the desk and said, "I'm Sharon Betters. Our son, Mark, has been in an accident." While hugging Sharon, I watched for the direction the nurse turned as she led us to Mark. I knew if she turned to the right, she was taking us to our son and that he was still alive. If she turned to the left, she was taking us to what we pastors call the "death room." The nurse turned to the left.

I stopped the nurse, held my wife tightly, and said, "I know this routine. Is Mark dead?" She nodded yes. I asked, "Is Kelly dead?" She nodded yes again. Sharon began to scream, "No, no, no..." as she pounded on my chest. All I could do was to hold her tightly and absorb her beating.

Thus began the torturous test of the validity of everything in which we believed. Sharon says that she knew people would expect her, as a pastor's wife, to display great faith and trust in God, but her cry that night was, "God, I won't pretend to trust You. I need to *know* that everything I have taught and lived is true and real. I need to *know* that if someone says they see strength in me, it's because You did it, not because I worked it up."

One year into our grief journey, Sharon declared to me, "This is too hard. I wish I could walk away from my faith and just accept that God isn't real, that He isn't here, because trusting Him feels so much harder than not trusting Him. But I can't because of our kids. I don't want them to reject their faith."

Her comments puzzled me. "Sharon, why do you want our kids to trust God when you want to walk away from your faith?" I asked. She replied, "Because in my heart of hearts I know that the only hope our kids have of experiencing joy in life is to reconcile God's love with His sovereignty. If I conclude that He isn't sovereign, that He is untrustworthy, what hope do we have? As hard as it is for me to trust Him with this anguish, I want our kids to see me walking by faith to help them live with confidence that they can trust Him in the darkness."

Sharon shares her struggle to reconcile the sovereignty of God with His love, in her book, *Treasures in Darkness: A Grieving Mother Shares Her Heart*.[2] When writing her book became too hard and she wanted to quit, I encouraged her to write it for our grandchildren, so that when life isn't fair and hard times come, they will have a record of how their grandparents learned to trust God in the darkness. Perhaps her book, along with this one, will be a manual for preparing them to walk by faith.

Parents, we must find the balance of teaching our children to capture the magic of each new day while accepting that, in this world, we will have trouble. But we must not lose heart, because Jesus has overcome the world.

In closing, my passion in writing this book is to confront parents with the knowledge of how seriously God views their parenting and that He has given us a parenting manual in Proverbs. But more importantly, I am passionate for parents to realize how critical it is for them to own and live out their faith in order to pass on a legacy of faith. Parenting requires sacrifice, and not just in the purchases we make, such as buying a family van instead of the sports car, giving up family vacations in order to pay for Christian schools, or staying home to raise the kids instead of building a career. It's submitting our own hearts to God's Word first, submitting to His call to live a life of holiness, and believing that He is sovereign and we can trust Him—even, if not most of all, with our children.

The best way to satisfy our heart's desire to protect our children and prepare them for a life of purpose and eternal success in these uncertain times is clearly spelled out by our Creator:

The fear of the Lord is the beginning of knowledge, but fools despise wisdom and discipline... He who fears the Lord, has a secure fortress, and for his children it will be a refuge. (Proverbs 1:7; Proverbs 14:26)

Over forty years ago, Sharon and I sent out wedding invitations that included this Scripture:

Trust in the Lord with all your heart and lean not on your own understanding; in all your ways acknowledge him and he will make your paths straight. (Proverbs 3:5, 6)

Matthew 6:33 is our life verse and engraved on our wedding bands: *But seek first his kingdom and his righteousness and all these things will be given to you as well.*

When God gave us children, Deuteronomy 6:6 gave us clear parenting instructions:

"These commandments that I give you today are to be upon your hearts. Impress them on your children. Talk about them when you sit at home and when you walk along the road, when you lie down and when you get up. Tie them as symbols on your hands and bind them on your foreheads. Write them on the doorframes of your house and on your gates."

These Scriptures have withstood the test of time in directing our lives as we have attempted to raise our children to know, love and fear God. It is our passion that young parents will embrace these Biblical truths as their roadmap for raising their own children while remaining committed to passing on to their children the hidden treasures of Proverbs.

Teaching Moments

• Dealing with disillusionment successfully requires understanding and believing Romans 8:28: *And we know that in all things God works for the good of those who love him, who have been called according to his purpose.* Baking bread from scratch with your children is a fun way to teach your child the truth of this Scripture. Together, taste each ingredient as you add it to the bowl, i.e. flour, salt, eggs, baking powder, yeast, etc. Make a big deal about how nasty the ingredients taste. While you're kneading the dough, talk about how the ingredients have to be pounded and stretched before the dough can rise and then be placed into the hot oven. While you are sharing a piece of hot buttered bread, fresh from the oven, remind your child of how bad the ingredients tasted by themselves, of how the ingredients had to be pounded and then put through "fire" in order to produce such a delicious piece of bread. Then explain how "all things" in their lives might taste just as nasty as the flour and salt, but that God promises to mix all things together in a way that will produce good in his or her life. Encourage your child to identify difficult challenges (the bully, the irritating teacher, the failed test, etc.) and help them see how those "nasty ingredients" can be mixed together in the whole of their lives to produce something good.

• Reach back into your childhood and recall a game you can play with your child where you take turns sharing the happiest time in your life and the saddest time, or the most disappointing time (use discretion in what you, as an adult, share!). Perhaps a few of your sad times involved not getting invited to a birthday party, not getting picked for the baseball team, or your best friend not liking you anymore. Maybe you tried to do something special for your mom and ended up making a mess instead. Share how you felt and responded in these situations, what you wish you had done differently ("get up and go"?), and ask your child to do the same.

• Create safe environments for your children to share their disillusionments by implementing the exhortation of Deuteronomy 6:6: *"These commandments that I give you today are to be upon your hearts. Impress them on your children. Talk about them when you sit at home and when you walk along the road, when you lie down and when you get up. Tie them as symbols on your hands and bind them on your foreheads. Write them on the doorframes of your house and on your gates."* Write out how you will apply this Scripture to each day's challenges.

- Plan regular one-on-one times with each child. When our children were very small, Sharon spent one evening a week with each one where they could choose a fun activity before bedtime. They were too small to interact on a deep level, but this kind of personal attention while they are toddlers creates a bond that will later invite the trust of a preteen or adolescent. Use car time as an opportunity to build traditions that make a child feel safe, such as stopping at the same store for a snack after sports or music lessons.

---

[1] Reprinted with permission from *Treasures of Faith: Living Boldly in View of God's Promises by Chuck and Sharon Betters*, P & R Publishing, P.O. Box 817, Phillipsburg, New Jersey 08865-0817 (1999), pages 129–131)

[2] *Treasures in Darkness, A Grieving Mother Shares Her Heart* by Sharon W. Betters, P & R Publishing (2005), available through www.markinc.org and all bookstores.

Scripture References in Order of Appearance

All Scripture references are in the New International Version of the Bible unless otherwise noted.

John 8:44
Proverbs 12:22
Proverbs 6:16-17
Proverbs 6:18-19
Philippians 4:2-3
Hebrews 12:14-15
Micah 2:1
Isaiah 57:9
Romans 3:13-18
Philippians 4:4-7
Philippians 2:5-8
Romans 8:1-2
Proverbs 10:17
Proverbs 12:15
Proverbs 13:18
Proverbs 19:20
Proverbs 23:12

Chapter Six

Daniel 1:12
Daniel 6:7-8
Daniel 6:13
Daniel 6:20
Daniel 6:21-22
Daniel 6:25-28
Luke 22:31
1 Corinthians 10:13
Daniel 3:24-25
1 Peter 5:8
Proverbs 7:1-5
Proverbs 7:14-18
Matthew 5:27-30
Matthew 6:9-13
Luke 11:2-4
John 1:1, 14
Proverbs 4:20-22
Proverbs 4:25-27

Proverbs 7:14
Proverbs 7:16
Proverbs 5:3-6
Proverbs 7:19-20
Proverbs 1:7
Proverbs 7:21-23
Proverbs 5:9-14
Proverbs 13:24
Proverbs 22:15

Chapter Seven

Luke 14:15-23
Luke 14:18-20
Luke 14:21
Luke 14:22
Luke 14:23
Proverbs 8:1-4
Genesis 17:1-7
John 3:3
2 Samuel 12:15-23
Ephesians 1:7-12
Ephesians 1:12-14
Psalm 51:5
Romans 3:23
Ephesians 2:4-5
John 3:4
1 John 5:11-13
Romans 8:15-17
Ephesians 1:13-14
Romans 3:23-26
John 17:17
1 Corinthians 2:9
Romans 8:28-30
Psalm 90:4
Proverbs 8:1-4
Luke 14:15-24
Romans 9:19-21

Luke 14:24
1 John 1:9
Hebrews 11:6
Ephesians 4:17-32
Proverbs 22:15
Proverbs 8:5
Exodus 10:1-3
Hebrews 12:6
Proverbs 22:6
Proverbs 8:6
Proverbs 8:7-8
John 14:6
Hebrews 13:8
Proverbs 8:10-11
Genesis 42:21
Ezra 9:6
Ephesians 4:17-32

Chapter Eight
2 Corinthians 5:17
Proverbs 8:12-36
John 1:12-13
Proverbs 8:12
Genesis 3:15
John 14:15-17
1 Corinthians 2:16
1 Corinthians 2:14-15
Hebrews 4:14-16
Romans 8:26-27
Proverbs 8:13
1 Peter 5:8
Mark 15:34
Matthew 26:53
Proverbs 8:14
1 Corinthians 10:13
1 Peter 2:20-21
Isaiah 45:3

Joel 2:25
Matthew 24:1-8
Proverbs 8:15-16
Proverbs 8:17
1 John 4:10
Ephesians 1:4
2 Thessalonians 2:13-1
John 15:16
Jeremiah 31:3
Isaiah 64:6
Matthew 5:48
Romans 3:23
Proverbs 8:18-21
1 Peter 1:4-5
Proverbs 8:22-31
Colossians 1:15-18
Proverbs 8:32-36

Chapter Nine
Proverbs 9:1
Ephesians 5:21-32
Revelation 1:4
1 Corinthians 15:12-19
John 16:7
John 17:24
Acts 2:1-3
John 14:23-26
Isaiah 1:18
Proverbs 9:2-3
Proverbs 9:4-6
Matthew 28:19-20

Chapter Ten
Proverbs 9:7-8
Proverbs 9:13-18
1 Timothy 1:13
Acts 13:45-46, 50

Matthew 7:6
Colossians 4:5-6
Isaiah 55:10-11
Proverbs 9:13
Proverbs 9:14-16
Proverbs 9:17
Proverbs 9:18
Ezekiel 18:20
Ephesians 6:1-4

Conclusion

Genesis 50:20
Proverbs 9:10-12
Proverbs 1:7
Acts 9:1-6
Proverbs 15:33
Proverbs 14:15
Proverbs 16:9
Proverbs 14:26-27
Proverbs 1:7
Proverbs 14:26
Proverbs 3:5-6
Deuteronomy 6:6
Romans 8:28

About the Author

Dr. Chuck Betters, an ordained pastor since 1969, has served in a variety of cultural settings including the inner city during the seventies. Chuck likes to say he cut his teeth in ministry on the streets of Philadelphia. For his entire career he has focused on not only the "thus says the Lord" aspects of Scripture but also the "so what" of Scripture–the practical exercise of Biblical truth. Chuck's uncompromising style has led thousands over the years to appreciate his holistic approach to Biblical preaching and teaching–what Chuck likes to call the "blue denim and lace" balance between the truth (logos) of the Scriptures, its ethical demands (ethos), and the great passion (pathos) with which he presents it.

Chuck and his wife, Sharon, have been married since 1969. They have four children. Their youngest son, Mark, was safely deposited in heaven when he was killed in a car accident in 1993. Chuck says of this tragedy that, "God, in His sovereignty, scorched my life in such a way that He unbolted me from my love affair with this world." Their two older sons, Chuck and Dan, serve in full-time pastoral ministry on the staff where Chuck is the Senior Pastor of the Glasgow Reformed Presbyterian Church (PCA) in Glasgow, Delaware. Their only daughter, Heidi, is a mother to five children and serves as the event coordinator for MARKINC Ministries, the media arm of Chuck's preaching and teaching ministry. Chuck and Sharon have 14 grandchildren. It is to these precious jewels that Chuck has dedicated this book in the hope and prayer that, as adults, they will embrace the great Proverbs of Scripture this book espouses and that their parents are teaching them. Chuck often says that the development of a successful spiritual legacy will not be fully realized until we see what kind of children our children raise. *Teaching Them Young* is Chuck's special contribution to his children's efforts in this great spiritual journey.

More exciting and inspirational resources from MARKINC Ministries...

Books

Treasures in Darkness:
A Grieving Mother Shares Her Heart
by Sharon Betters

Treasures of Encouragement:
Women Helping Women
in the Church
by Sharon Betters

Treasures of Faith:
Living Boldly in View of
God's Promises
Guide
by Charles and Sharon Betters

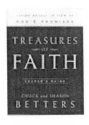

Treasures of Faith:
Living Boldly in View of
God's Promises - A Leader's

by Charles and Sharon Bet-

Visit www.markinc.org for ordering information!

More exciting and inspirational resources from MARKINC Ministries...

CDs

Learning to See When the Lights Go Out series

Alcoholism: Hope and Help

Dying with Dignity and Grace

Autism Spectrum Disorders: Speaking Hope Healers

First Responders: Wounded

Terminal Illness

Coming Home from War

Visit www.markinc.org for ordering information!